# FAST FORWARD

copyright© 2010 by FF>> Press

All rights reserved. Except for brief passages quoted in newspaper, magazine, radio or television review, no part of this publication may be published, reproduced, performed, distributed, or transmitted in any forms of media, or by any other means electronic or mechanical including photocopy, recording or any information storage and retrieval system now known or to be invented, without permission in writing from the authors, their authorized agents or heirs.

Published by FF>> Press.

ISBN: 978-0-9817852-2-6

Library of Congress Control Number: 2010927946

cover design: Stacy Walsh
typesetting/layout design: M.D'Alessandro

# FAST FORWARD
## THE MIX TAPE
a collection of flash fiction
*Volume 3*

**EDITED BY**
K. Scott Forman
Kona Morris
& Nancy Stohlman

FF>> Press 2010

# CONTENTS

*foreword* — vii

## SIDE A:
## I BROUGHT THE CHEETOS BUT I FORGOT MY SOUL

| | |
|---|---|
| POST-INDUSTRIAL LOVE >> *Alexander Weinstein* | 1 |
| CROSSING THE BORDER >> *Ian Hunter* | 5 |
| THE STORY OF HOW... >> *Travis Macdonald* | 8 |
| OMITTED EXCERPT >> *Alexander Weinstein* | 9 |
| THE BROKEN HOUSE OF NANJING >> *Matt Siegel* | 12 |
| MAGIC PALM >> *Kevin Brown* | 14 |
| NOMINATIVE DESTINY >> *Gloria Frym* | 17 |
| ONE OF THESE DAYS >> *Frank P Galiani* | 20 |
| CANDLELIGHT >> *Christy Strick* | 22 |
| A SMALL DISTRACTION >> *Jarod Rosello* | 24 |
| LIKE CLUMPS OF DRIED DIRT >> *Bryan Jansing* | 26 |
| LI'L JAMIE >> *Robert McGowan* | 28 |
| DANCERS >> *Christy Strick* | 30 |
| VODKA AND ICE >> *Charles Rutter* | 32 |
| BEETLE >> *Zach Andrews* | 33 |
| THE SOWER >> *Jesse Goolsby* | 36 |
| PRELUDE TO A KISS >> *Erik Morsink* | 40 |
| BRIDGE PARTY >> *Bryan Jansing* | 44 |

| | |
|---|---|
| IN MEXICO >> *Teresa Milbrodt* | 48 |
| LEADER OF MEN >> *Meg Tuite* | 51 |
| BREAKFAST >> *Lee Griffith* | 53 |
| ANOTHER CHEESE RUN >> *Mark Fallon* | 56 |
| WHERE'D THE CHEESE GO? >> *Jason Sinclair Long* | 58 |
| CHEESE >> *Natania Rosenfeld* | 59 |
| LIGHTNING WATCH >> *Dustin M. Hoffman* | 63 |
| THE STORM >> *Curtis Smith* | 65 |
| MARGE >> *Devin Murphy* | 67 |
| HERE IN THIS >> *Faye Kicknosway* | 70 |
| DEAD AND ALIVE >> *Michael Spring* | 73 |
| OBLIVIOUS TO THE INCREASINGLY... >> *Travis Macdonald* | 75 |
| THE THINGS WE TAKE AND THE THINGS WE LEAVE BEHIND >> *Ashley Cowger* | 76 |
| THIRD STREET >> *April Johnston* | 80 |
| THE KNIFE >> *Robin Hillard* | 82 |
| CATASTROPHE >> *Robin Hillard* | 85 |
| FORTY >> *Michael Dean Clark* | 88 |
| THINGS I SHOULD HAVE TOLD HER BEFORE SHE LEFT >> *Ray Morrison* | 93 |
| THE WHISPER IN THE CHURCH, FLICKER OF THE CANDLE THERE >> *Chris Bowen* | 95 |
| THE SIXTH QUEEN, CATHERINE PARR >> *Sophie Rosenblum* | 97 |
| THE BATHTUB >> *Brian Seemann* | 98 |
| NOTES ON JESUS >> *Teresa Milbrodt* | 102 |
| CLOWNING FOR JESUS >> *Nancy Stohlman* | 105 |
| MR. NASTY >> *Robert Scotellaro* | 108 |
| THE HAND MODEL >> *Dawn Sueoka* | 112 |
| FLOWERS FROM CHARLIE ROSE >> *Liam McAuliffe* | 114 |
| SUMMER SNOW >> *Charles Rutter* | 118 |
| WE FELT BURDENED BY IT >> *Sophie Rosenblum* | 119 |
| A TERRIER'S LIMITS >> *Sophie Rosenblum* | 120 |
| ANIMAL CONTROL >> *Nick Sansone* | 121 |
| IN THE PARK >> *Félix Calvino* | 123 |
| BALANCING RACKS >> *Jason Sinclair Long* | 125 |
| HOW THE PARKING AUTHORITY RUINED MY SATURDAY NIGHT >> *April Johnston* | 126 |
| CONFESSION #3 >> *Kona Morris* | 128 |
| LUST AND DUST IN THE AFTERNOON >> *Gene Twaronite* | 129 |
| THE FIRST TIME >> *Susan Lewis* | 131 |
| HEISENBERG'S SALON >> *Susan Lewis* | 133 |
| THE APOCALYPSE TALES: LAURA RECEIVES A RESPONSE >> *Alexander Weinstein* | 135 |

# FOREWORD
## the mix tape

I used to be a master mix tape maker. I passed many satisfying evenings gluing *Onion* headlines to tape cases as I recorded my journeys through favorite songs, stories, emotions, preferences, and random associations.

Unlike their less cool cousins—mix cd's—a mix tape was an investment of time and attention from the creator, who had to stay present during its creation like a radio dj, cuing each song, trying to avoid too much lag between them. Dancing or singing or laughing along in real time. As each song etched itself onto the tape, you remembered why you loved it and why your future listener was going to love it, a collection of private jokes and history between you. Feeling your way through the moods and storylines of the music, you knew intuitively whether it was time for Bob Dylan or time for The Cure, whether Tom Waits could follow Tori Amos (and what can possibly follow Tom Waits)?

Being a prolific mix tape maker, I also used to receive them in return, little mementos and expressions of friends that I kept in a tape case in my old beater car that I bought for $200, the one that I kept blankets in because it didn't have heat, until that night a cowboy broke in during a rainstorm and stole the tape case—only the tape case—then growled at me from under his 10-gallon hat as I tried to chase him across the street (true story). But sometimes now, I'll still come across one of those remaining mix tapes and blow the dust off the tape player—five opening notes and I am instantly transported back to say, 1992, and the taste of Snapple, C & C Music Factory. Or to 1996 and that summer in Georgia with Janis Joplin and Ray Charles, that summer when everyone was playing Alanis Morrisette and I was young and still too shy to call myself a writer.

Fast forward to 2010. Faced with the overwhelming task and great honor of arranging the stories in Fast Forward's third flash fiction anthology, I was reminded of the joys of making those old mix tapes, a task I haven't embarked since my "Saturn Returns Mix" nearly a decade ago.

So I wrote each of the stories on a flash card. Then I got the requisite drink, smoke, comfortable pillow, and spread the stories over every inch of my living room as I would have my music long ago. Funny the patterns that started emerging, like beetles, cockroaches, cheese, Jesus… an apocalyptic pizza parlor spread out before me. Stylistic themes emerged too, stories told in one long breathless sentence, stories told through numbered lists, ultra flash stories (under 100 words).

I began Side One with "Post Industrial Love" by Alexander Weinstein, a delightfully abstract piece that kicks off the FF Mix Tape with smirky mischievousness. From there I allowed the stories to surf between funny and poignant, long and short, through novels, bugs, Europe, horny dogs, and topless pancakes. We play voyeur to a multitude of couples, watching the difficult beauty of intimacy and relationships, then head into religion, clowns, hired Disney characters and other confessions, and then finish in the weird wasteland of inanimate objects, including robots, cars, and even, in "Heisenberg's Salon" by Susan Lewis, whole apartments, with self-determination and a sense of humor.

By Side Two the task had overtaken me... I was recognizing the random connections, silly juxtapositions and chilling moments broken only by little blips like Travis Macdonald's brilliant micro stories, one of which, "Everyone Enjoyed the Buffett," begins Side Two with dark comedy. The B-Side dips into poignant and often darker areas of human experience, including funerals, poverty, the Holocaust... the mood seesaws from dark to light, from faded queens and superheros, teen pregnancies and eating disorders to freaky fairy tales and mythological creatures and finally hitting one of the collection's darkest pieces, "The Red Road" by Toyin Odewunmi. Then, as Side Two and the entire Mix Tape begins its final climb towards denouement, we take one last detour through the abstract, through chicken trees and apple trees and bearded women and finally end with "Jesus at the Diner" by J.P. Vallieres, a story that reminds us that our lives can be as consequential or inconsequential as we make them.

And then you flip the tape over and begin again. So enjoy these stories alone or rewind to the beginning of Side One and go along for the full ride. Like those mix tapes of old, take it as a special homemade message from our hearts to yours.

*Nancy Stohlman, March 3, 2010*

# POST-INDUSTRIAL LOVE
*Alexander Weinstein*

I awoke that morning to a horrendous noise, and believed a creature with a face of a thousand drills was devouring a steel beam. I got out of bed, walked to my bathroom window, and parted the curtains. In the parking lot I saw a group of men in plastic yellow suits destroying my car. One of them was driving a bulldozer with an enormous drill bit attached to it. He positioned the drill in the center of the sunroof. The other men yelled things like, "All right, you got it," and "Go ahead." Then the awful noise of the machine started up again and the drill chewed into my car, spitting metal and upholstery all over the gravel.

"What kind of bullshit is this?" I thought and went to get my jacket and shoes on.

This was the reason I arrived fifteen minutes late to the restaurant and, in turn, why my friend Roger won't return my calls anymore. Roger's the type of guy who, if you take him to the zoo, can't help but yell inappropriate things at the animals like, "Come and try to get my wallet, you asshole!" In short, not always the easiest guy to get along with. He was annoyed that I was late and wouldn't accept my excuse. We shared a plate of General Tso's chicken in silence.

The main problem was that when I needed a wooden coat rack most, Roger wouldn't help. Roger has a number of high quality wooden coat racks that he's always lent me when I needed them, provided I return them to him after getting back from the airport. He had an assortment with him at the restaurant that day but said that, given my tardiness, he "couldn't bring himself to part with them." Which meant I was left up the creek without a coat rack when I needed it most. My fiancé was arriving from Denver that afternoon.

Having a coat rack to hang her jacket on as soon as she got off the airplane was of ultimate importance to my fiancé. During intimate moments she'd related how her parents never brought coat racks to the airport and how deeply that had affected her. I was the only boyfriend that had ever cared enough. Ever since increased security she'd been forced to wait until she got to the baggage terminal to hang her coat. I always made a point to be there waiting with one. Admittedly, it would've been wise to have a coat rack of my own, but Roger was always forthcoming with his. A hanger was out of the question. There's something frightening, almost criminal, about appearing in public with a hanger. A wooden coat rack, on the other hand, carries an air of respectability.

My fiancé was already at baggage claim, her coat in a pile by her feet, when I arrived. Her mascara was streaked with tears.

"Where's the coat rack?" she asked as I gave her a kiss.

"I'm sorry, Roger didn't give me his."

"Roger's a jerk! Look at my coat!"

I picked her coat from the floor and hung it over my arm. It looked pathetic hanging like that.

"Why weren't you here on time?"

"I'm sorry, some men came and destroyed my car this morning."

"Oh my God."

"It's okay, they were from the city."

"Oh." She wiped her tears with a tissue. "Well, I brought you something from Denver." She picked up a plastic pet carrier from the floor. Inside I could make out the black and white fur of a small cat.

"Hi, kitty," I said poking my finger through the wire door.

"Get your finger out of there! It's a Tasmanian Devil. They can bite through bone in seconds."

I pulled my finger back out.

"I thought you might want to name him Lou."

"That's my name," I said.

"I know. I thought you could learn something from him."

It was then I realized something had changed in my fiancé. She was acting too sweet. Never had she brought me back presents from a trip and here she was suddenly giving me a Tasmanian Devil. On the shuttle ride home it came out.

"I like Denver," she told me. She turned towards me. "I'm tired of being together with you. I want to live somewhere that has more homeless people."

"There are homeless people by the co-op," I said.

"The co-op has an awful hot bar."

I couldn't argue with that. Sometimes they try to expand their choices from rice, beans, sautéed vegetables, and grilled tempeh, but it's true, it's really pretty boring. I promised I'd put in a comment card.

"Jeez, Lou, you just don't get it do you?" she said. And I didn't. But for a moment, as the shuttle drove us down the highway, the billboards going by behind her, I saw my fiancé as I always wanted to remember her: Her face highlighted by the fluorescent lights of the shuttle, the sound of Lou crunching through the buffalo wings we'd bought him, and the fleeting phrase, "Ask What Geico Can Do For You" speeding past on a billboard.

# CROSSING THE BORDER
## *Ian Hunter*

I could hear the dog behind us, barking over the noise of the engine. Penny looked anxiously out of the back window.

"It's gaining."

I nodded, weaving my way through roads and streets that seemed unfamiliar to me, as if I did not recognise the arrangement of buildings we passed. At least the train stations looked familiar.

"Look out!" Penny cried as a giant silver boot fell out of the sky and landed beside us.

I swerved and glanced up, huge dark shapes moved overhead, blurred by thick bands of clouds.

Suddenly the car stalled.

"It's coming."

She was right. The silver dog was gaining on us, relentless, filling up my rear view mirror.

I twisted the ignition key and crunched the gears before we roared off, leaving the dog in our wake. We sped round the corner and I could sense the border up ahead, round one more turn, the place where riches lay.

If we got that far.

Then I heard sirens. A cop on a motorbike drew nearer, then level, gesturing for me to pull over.

I stopped the car and heard Penny rummaging in her handbag.

"Okay, you know the drill," the cop said, opening his notebook. "Do not—"

Penny flipped the card towards him. His face turned sour as he read it.

"Lucky you," he muttered. "I haven't seen one of those for years. Go on, beat it."

"Here comes the dog again," said Penny. She flinched as she glanced up through the sunroof. "And the boot."

I nodded, feeling the ground shake as the boot hit the slick road surface next to us.

We zoomed off, heading for the pay off spot, but the dog was gaining, face cracked open to reveal a silvery grin.

"Slow down," Penny warned.

No way I was going to let the dog beat me. I licked my lips as the right-angle turn got nearer.

"We'll never make it," she warned, voice rising.

I changed down, jabbed the brakes, and yanked the steering wheel round as far as I could. The car slid across the road then straightened, roaring across the border.

I slowed slightly, and rolled down my window. Someone put 200 bucks into my outstretched hand.

"We're rich," said Penny.

"Not yet," I told her. "We still have a long way to go."

Licking my lips, I pressed on the accelerator,

taking us down the road towards another of those 90 degree turns, while brightly coloured hotels and houses appeared on either side of us, like the blooming of strange flowers.

# THE STORY OF HOW WE ALL WAITED IN QUIET AND PIOUS ANTICIPATION FOR SEVERAL HOURS ON END AS OUR SO-CALLED SAVIOR FEASTED ON THE WORLDLY PRAISES OF OUR MORTAL SWORN ENEMIES AND LAUGHED WITH THEM AT OUR EXPENSE

*Travis Macdonald*

Then it rained and we all went back to work on our novels.

# OMITTED EXCERPT
*Alexander Weinstein*

This morning I awoke to the realization that I'd been living my life within a parenthetical statement. The discovery of my parentheticality gave way to a second, more disheartening realization: I was not alone. For it seemed to me there were many people who felt the way I did. People who, having realized they were living within parenthesis, mitigated their melancholy by placing others within their own set of parenthesis (K-Mart cashiers, telemarketers, auto mechanics, etcetera (and that these individuals, had their own substrata of parenthetical individuals, ad infinitum). It was a pathetic situation, more so since I'd suddenly become aware of how trapped I was within my own punctuation.[1]

---

1. And while I may have my private moments, my mental footnotes as it were (like how on Sunday evenings I enjoy drawing myself a bath, lighting some candles, putting on Coltrane's *Crescent* and slipping away), even these footnotes were still within the parenthetical realm.

They say the first step to overcoming depression is realizing you are in fact depressed. Being within parenthesis, however, is an odd state that feels hopelessly disconnected. One is, of course, part of the larger something, but what that something is remains unknown, sealed off by crescent shaped punctuation. Within this state it's easy to reflect on one's ultimate insignificance to the main story, and I'll admit it, to consider editing oneself out completely.

That was not the way I wished to go, a deleted series of inconsequential sentences. Regardless of my narrative status, I still believe I have potential to exist outside parenthesis. Even if my mark is to be merely a footnote at the end of a long sentence, I have a calling within the larger story of life.[2] It's hard to maintain hope though. One gets the feeling that, outside, all sorts of marvelous events are occurring. When I climb to the top of the tallest T in this sentence I can see over the walls of my confinement. There are indeed people out there doing things, falling in love, raising children, fully engaged in the stories of their lives. There is one man in particular who stops to pet a woman's dog, and as he bends over in the middle of a country road at dusk, there's a sense of true non-parenthetical beauty.

I climb down from my T and am consoled only by my own company and the cramped space of my dwelling. Over the walls of my parenthesis the sun is setting. Dusk casts its light along the edges of my small compartment and then is gone. I turn on the lights and open the fridge. There are a couple slices

---

2. And when that time comes, my footnote won't be one contained within punctuation reachable only by momentary Shifts.

of pizza (delivered, I guiltily admit, by a man I placed into my own parenthesis). I eat the cold slices and turn on the water in the bathtub.

As I slip into the warm claw-foot, I momentarily escape my confines. In these moments I dream I am leaning out the tallest tower of a castle. Far below I see the walls of my parenthesis, small and insignificant as ellipses. As candles flicker off bathroom tiles, and Coltrane plays in the footnotes, I dream myself free.)[3]

---

3.

# THE BROKEN HOUSE OF NAN-JING
*Matt Siegel*

Dr. Jian Hsing, a Chinese professor of history, used to sit out on his back deck in the morning light and work on his manuscript, a memoir about growing up in Nanjing decades after the massacre. He'd sift through photos of disemboweled women, young girls bayoneted through lower orifices, charred bodies left without remorse, he'd read through transcripts of an American reporter who described the streets so strewn with bodies that one had no choice but to drive over them to reach the safety zone, and he'd found an interview with a woman who survived days of near-constant gang rape and nearly a dozen bayonets through her chest and neck before being found, nearly lifeless, by passersby and nursed back to a state of health checked by scars, disability, and venereal disease.

When he was finished with his fourth draft and sitting on a growing pile of rejection letters, he asked the administration if he could read a chapter in the central quad, and they set up a podium twenty yards from a group of sorority girls selling raffle tickets for an all-expense paid trip to Cabo. But few looked and fewer listened. The sorority girls' solicitous screams drowned out talk of rape and mutilation and Japanese denial and omission from history books, and a circle of friends joked behind cigarettes while cell-phoned students crossed the professor's back and front on their way to class.

The professor returned home and fell into a depression. He stopped going to work. Stopped going anywhere. And several weeks later, when his neighbors mailed him a letter asking him to mow his lawn, he responded by distributing his collection of transcribed notes and postmortem photographs to their mailboxes. When they didn't respond he distributed the full manuscript, and when they mailed a second letter informing him that his use of their mailboxes was a violation of federal law and asking him to please mow his lawn, the professor took a machete to his bushes, a hammer to his mailbox, rocks to his windows, and a crowbar to his roof—where he lost his footing trying to peel up shingles, and fell beside his mutilated bushes.

He came back from the ER with a line of stitches, a concussion, and a leg cast—but not before making friends with the physician who treated him: a Japanese man called Chiyuu, whose wife, Susan, a fledgling assistant at a New York publishing house, got her first break weeks later with the acquisition of Jian Hsing's memoir: *The Broken House of Nanjing*.

# **MAGIC PALM**
## (for mei...)
### *Kevin Brown*

An angel, Grandmother would say, saved her life during a four-story suicide jump the year China went Red. Me on her lap, she told how she toed the ledge, stared out at the network of alleyways smothered in smoke and screams and men tearing through men. How she leaned forward and the landscape fell up, toward and past her. How Kuan Shih Yin, the Goddess of Mercy, appeared and placed a palm beneath her. Whispered, "The Earth shall keep spinning. Spin with it," and eased her to the ground. "I broke a leg and both arms," she said, raising two gnarled fingers, "but it was magical."

I'd cry when she told me about Grandfather, whom she hadn't seen since the day he was taken away. He'd been a politician in the Nationalist Government, and so imprisoned for life. "They took my possessions," she said, "then my husband. Forced me to bow and confess against him to avoid his immediate execution." She'd stare ahead. "Last time I heard his voice, he was screaming mine and your mother's names as they drug him away." She'd blink several times and I could see the image dissipating, melting into the now. "We were helpless in a country that needed help," she said. "Unable to save those who needed saving."

Years later, we returned to the location of her old house, but it was gone, replaced by an office building. Grandmother only smiled and said, "Prettier than it used to be."

She died shortly after. As she was lowered into the ground, I asked Mother if she believed a Deva really saved her.

"I don't *not* believe it," Mother said.

I was married later that year, and each time I looked at my husband, I'd think of Grandmother's story. How hard it must've been to have everything one second, and be bowing as it is dragged away the next. How easy it'd be to jump. How hard to climb down.

So I mentally recorded my husband's voice, his smells. Behind my eyes, I imprinted his shape and face. Then, on June 4th, 1989, he was killed in Tiananmen Square, when a tank rolled between us and has never moved since.

A week later, I stood on my own four-story ledge with a bottle of prescription pills. Toed the edge and looked out at my mental vision of the world, a network of alleyways that all led to the same dead end. At everyone helpless in a country that needed help. I missed my husband. Wanted to see Grandmother arm-in-arm with Grandfather, the memories of forced bows and screams erased forever. So I jumped by swallowing every pill. Felt the landscape fall up, toward and past me, until my angel, *my* Goddess of Mercy, my grandmother appeared, and placed a withered palm beneath me. Whispered: "The world shall keep spinning. Spin with it," and eased me to the ground, where I vomited and it was magical.

# **NOMINATIVE DESTINY**
## *Gloria Frym*

After the minister told the wedding guests that the new bride came from Adam's rib, the mother of the groom, Mrs. Arden, praised the lord for not delivering rain that evening. *Thank you so much*, she beamed, *I present you with the new Mrs. Arden,* but not before Ms. Gordon, mother of Annabelle Dutton, attended a PTA meeting only to discover there was no nametag for her because Mrs. Dutton, new wife of Mr. Dutton, father of Annabelle Dutton, was assumed parent of Annabelle by the president of the PTA since Mrs. Dutton recently gave birth to Clarkson Kently Dutton, the president nearly apoplectic that a volunteer must have made a clerical error in failing to list Ms. Gordon as Annabelle's mother whose own mother née Potts assumed the name Gordon as soon as she could to escape the potty jokes she and her father before her had suffered as a child, when the elder Mr. Gordon was best friends with Tom Pearlman whose son changed his name to Paxton to secure a job in advertising, whose niece's close friend changed his name from John Davis to Max Greenstreet who married a woman who gladly changed her last name with him, and when their computer servers went on the blink they became telephone acquaintances with Bob from Bangladesh, Mary from Mumbai, Jane from Jallalabad, who went by no last names, similar to Zorro or Prince and Madonna and Beyoncé and Ludacris and characters in Kafka whose Joseph K is simply K for three hundred pages, or A Hunger Artist with no name at all, so unlike Garcia Lorca or Garcia Marquez to honor both gene pools, and then there are the Russian names where a simple Marina in one short story can be variously referred to as Marisha, Marinochka, Marissa or even Marishka, confusing the reader as to who waits in the parlour nervously stroking her dog Masha, which is nothing compared to patronymics and matronymics of those five fictional aristocratic families the Bezukhovs, the Bolkonskys, the Rostovs, the Kuragins and the Drubetskoys who lived in Moscow or St. Petersburg which became Stalingrad then St. Petersburg again, unlike Hot Springs, New Mexico permanently renamed Truth or Consequences, or T or C to the locals, after a 50s radio show host announced that he would air the program from the first city that renamed itself after the quiz show, and every May holds a beauty contest and a parade that features royalty such as Maria Martinez, the Chile Queen of Hatch, vaguely related to the Duchess of Alba, married to Luis Martinez de Irujo, whose daughter Maria Eugenia Brianda Timotea Cecilia Martinez de Irujo y Fitz-James Stuart frequently scandalizes the society pages, himself son of the Duke of Sotomayor whose second Duke of Alba in 1492 signed the capitulation of Granada, and let's not get into Chinese names where every writer has a pseudonym such as Zhang Er the poet, who is also called Mingxia Li the medical ethicist, or noms de guerre exemplified by Carlos the Jackal and Sid Vicious, and we all lived through Patty morphing into Tanya and back to Patty again, and Fatdog who is currently known as Fatty, and Subcomandante Marcos whose given name may be unknown, and Malcolm X who converted to Malik El-Shabazz, and all the Pope John Pauls or should it be Johns Paul, what about George Foreman's five sons named George Jr., George III, George IV, George V and George VI, and all those Louis' with their gilded furniture, so obverse to the great Jamaica Kinkaid who writes books but didn't when she was Elaine Cynthia Richardson, surely George Eliot thought more deeply than Mary Anne Evans, and George Sand could smoke cigars whereas Aurore Dupin wore stays, and Vostanik Manoog Adoyan invented Arshille Gorky, after Samuel Langhorne Clemens adopted Mark Twain, and another American dream was born out of Norma Jean, and Moon Unit dropped the Unit and Chief Sitting Bull or "Jumping Badger" as a boy also nicknamed "Slow" because he took extra time to do things, and was there really every Tom Dick and Harry ever?

# ONE OF THESE DAYS
*Frank P. Galiani*

One of these days I'll get the recognition that I so richly, albeit modestly, deserve, whether that so far unawarded recognition values me as a politician, for I have been renowned in my time both in the House of Commons, and later, when I finally came into my true station, for my service in the House of Lords, alongside, I might remind you, my friend of many years, and I would hasten to add, famous in his own, if limited, position, and, whose name I must be careful not to admit (but no doubt you will have already guessed), Benjamin Disraeli, however, probably due to my innate modesty I might, (or might not), have omitted to mention, even though history has chosen to remember that name, although not always, and not only as a politician, or, as I would prefer to refer to my service to my country but by another sobriquet, as a leader and statesman, not only as an honored peer of the country upon which the sun will never set, but also as a lord of the admiralty, which I would have been had I chosen to accept the honored appointment from Lord Melbourne, then Prime Minister, which I declined because that venerable position would likely have interfered with my activities as an author, which decision, I'm sure, would have caused great distress to many of the "great unwashed," a colorful term which I, I must admit modestly, first introduced to our mother tongue in my 1834 novel, *The Last Days of Pompeii*, which being but one of my twenty-three published novels, well acclaimed (perhaps too well acclaimed, for was not my 1830 novel *Paul Clifford*, though appearing on the British scene four years earlier, not to become the one which gave me lasting fame and acclaim), although some doubters and naysayers, blackguards though they may be, insultingly refer to it as infamy, as if they had ever produced better writing, my greatness also evidenced by another deathless phrase which I introduced in my 1839 play *Richelieu*, that phrase being, as surely every schoolboy knows, "beneath the rule of men entirely great, the pen is mightier than the sword," which as I see you snap your fingers in sudden recognition, I sit back with a smug, but not offensively so, sneer of satisfaction, for it is a wondrous great feeling to receive, if belatedly, recognition for my genius, although my apt phrase, "pursuit of the almighty dollar," has yet to receive the recognition, and I daresay acclaim, that any reasonable, if modest, intellectual, would rightfully expect, though I have not seen it, or at least not to the extent that I would, modestly, hope, even though I do expect to experience it at some time in the near future, because I do truly believe that one of these days you will surely recognize the name Edward George Earle Lytton Bulwer-Lytton, 1st Baron Lytton, but it will probably not be until a dark and stormy night.

# CANDLELIGHT
*Christy Strick*

Like a candle left burning through the night, her mother's face is melting in upon itself, puddling at her neck, the neck that had once smelled of Chanel and Dove soap, that had held a tear-drenched face against it many times over the years, as the years slowly melted away from them, she and her sister and their mother, the mother that raised them and shouted at them to clean up after themselves and then did the cleaning herself, who did everything herself, cooking and cleaning and washing and scolding and working, working in an office for a man who brushed himself against her because she was a woman alone, a woman without a man, and that made her easy in his eyes, and in the eyes of his wife, who insisted that she be let go, and then where was she to go but to K-mart, where the hours were long and hard and sometimes she'd get home too late to tuck her girls into bed, they'd have fed themselves and bathed themselves and gone to bed, told each other stories of fairy princesses, held on to each other when a noise made them think of the father who used to stand outside the house shouting at their mother to let him in, let him in, it was his goddamned house after all, and she'd never make it without him, didn't she know that a woman needed a man, and who else would want her anyway, but then there were plenty of men who wanted her, wanted that soft sweet Chanel and Dove scented neck to nuzzle against, wanted everything but gave nothing, until finally none wanted her anymore as her face melted and puddled itself at her neck and she could no longer clean or cook or wash or scold or work and when the flame sputters and finally goes out, there are only her daughters to see and to notice the darkness.

# A SMALL DISTRACTION
## Jarod Rosello

He is about to fall asleep, or thinks he's about to fall asleep, feels that sort of weightless feeling that comes right before sleep and has his eyes closed and his head on the pillow and the blanket over him and the lights off and all that—ready for sleep—and he lies there waiting for sleep, but it doesn't come, because while all the conditions are right—the environment and even the time of night—his mind is a little too awake. He feels physically tired but not mentally, and so he's pretty sure he's not going to be able to sleep, even if he lies here for a while, even if he gives it an hour or so. Besides, he's heard that if you want to sleep and can't, trying to sleep is the worst thing you can do. He should walk around, watch some television, maybe read something, go for a light run around the block but it's late so maybe just jog up and down the hallway, do a few pull ups, make a sandwich, fix the leg on the table in the living room. He gets out of bed and just stands for a moment. He scratches the back part of his arm, not his forearm, but the part behind the bicep—he doesn't know what that part of the arm is called. He scratches there and feels a small bump and picks at it and it eventually comes off in his fingers, and he looks at it and notices that it's something small and black, and so he looks more closely at it, puts his glasses on and gets a good look, and sees that it's an insect, a tick, he thinks. He throws it onto the ground, worried it was burrowing into his fingers—if that's what they do. He gets back on the bed, then looks on the floor, finds it. Definitely a tick, the legs all moving. Very small. Could be one of those that carries Lyme disease. And it was in him, right in his arm, he had to dig it out. It did come out more easily than he thought a tick would come out, so maybe it hadn't really dug in there well. He takes his shoe, says, "I'm sorry for this tick, I don't usually like to kill anything, even disease-carrying ticks," and crushes it on the floor. He lifts the shoe and sees that the tick is still moving, still squirming its legs about, so he brings the shoe down again. It's still alive. He says, "I'm sorry this is taking so long," and he does one more time, but this time he wipes the shoe across the floor, and when he lifts it again, the tick is smeared onto the shoe. He didn't see a lot of blood—the tick didn't seem gorged—so maybe it hadn't really gotten in him well, hadn't sucked much blood or any at all. He does a quick check of his body, places he thinks ticks might be: under his arms, his legs, pubic area, his hairline. After a while he feels like there are probably no other ticks on him, and he gets back in bed, back under the covers as he was before, head on the pillow, light off, eyes closed, and waits just a second, just a half-second even, and falls asleep.

# LIKE CLUMPS OF DRIED DIRT
## *Bryan Jansing*

The dirt explodes into fragmented pebbles as she throws clumps from the pot to the concrete like mini grenades.

"Dirt, dada, dirt."

"Yeah honey, dirt."

The scattered shards of dry dirt send the scout ants into a frenzy as they scramble to relocate their chemical paths.

"Fuzz dada, fuzz."

"No honey, they're ants. It's okay, they won't hurt you."

"Okay."

She marvels at them, then gouges them from existence with a green penny she's found in the earth. He's about to reprimand her but closes his dry mouth. Who cares. A survivor shakes and vibrates to get all six legs to move in sync, to shimmy away from an unconscionable two year old with a green penny.

When she returns to smash the quivering ant he

stops her.

"Let him be, honey. He's suffered enough."

"Fuzz."

"Yes honey, Fuzz."

Then she scrapes him from existence.

# LI'L JAMIE
## *Robert McGowen*

Li'l Jamie—he hates being called that; at seven, he's not a kid anymore—discovered a bug one morning in the bathroom when he opened the drawer where his toothpaste was. It scurried away to the back.

And then he saw why it was there.

In the drawer was an old bottle of maybe hand lotion or something that belonged to his mother, and the poor cockroach had been eating the label, scraping off tiny bits of it, living on paper and glue.

He felt sorry for it, having to be there in the dark all the time, practically starving to death.

He decided right then that he'd never tell his mother about this roach living in his toothpaste drawer. He knew what she'd do if she learned it was there and what it was doing, eating the label off that lotion bottle. She'd poison it.

But there was nothing good in the drawer for the roach to eat. There was no way it could be happy having to survive on paper and dried glue.

So Jamie started feeding the roach. Every day maybe a tiny speck of bread. Or two or three grains or so of oatmeal would be all. Or a cookie crumb sometimes, not often, but so that now and then the roach would have something sweet. Little pieces you could barely see so there'd be no chance his mother would notice—if she ever even went in that drawer, which she never did. Just little tiny bits. A cockroach couldn't eat very much. And sometimes, after he brushed his teeth, Jamie would flick a little drop of water from his toothbrush into the front corner of the drawer, next to whatever morsel of food he'd dropped there.

The roach ate most of what he left for it. Jamie monitored the situation faithfully, a responsibility he'd solemnly committed to, watching after the cockroach in his toothpaste drawer.

He fed the roach for most of a year. And then, seeing one day that its food was no longer being eaten, he searched for it and found it dead at the rear of the next drawer down.

So he picked it up by one of its spooky-long antennae and brought it over to the toilet and flushed it away, is what Li'l Jamie did.

# DANCERS
*Christy Strick*

The cockroach lies on its back, legs dancing wildly in the air. Ana's own long limbs once carried her across the stage, strong muscles kicking, leaping. They won't carry her a block now without cramping.

From her prone position, face hanging over the edge of the plastic-covered mattress, she can see every hairy section of the roach's jointed legs. Not unlike her own thin, unshaven ones. Her hand drops over the side of the bed.

Metal clanks against metal, and a shadow falls across the floor by Ana's face.

She lets the roach's legs brush against her palm before she closes her fingers and sits up on the bunk.

"I used to be a dancer," she says as she struggles to stand.

"Yeah, and I was Dirty Harry. Now I'm just a guard and you're just a junkie with three strikes. Let's go."

As she walks through the corridor, the orchestra begins, and in her fist, Mr. Roach waltzes. Gracefully, elegantly he moves with the rhythm of the music, and Ana feels him quiver as the string section wrings tears from violins and violas and cellos. She feels the music echo in her own muscles, and together they float, the ballerina and the roach, spinning and gliding, the world falling away until it becomes nothing more than a blur, a stage.

When the orchestra fades, the roach stills. Ana allows him a brief break, then, anxious for the performance to resume, shakes her hand, signaling the end of the intermission. The roach begins his finale, dancing frantically as the music rises to a pulsing crescendo, winds and strings and percussion instruments joining together, a cacophony of glorious, beautiful notes. Ana feels the sweet familiar rush, lets the thrashing legs in her palm and the drumming in her pulse lead her, carry her, sweep her up and away.

They spend themselves, finally. The music in Ana and in the roach goes silent.

At the door to the courtroom, Ana kneels. She opens her hand and drops the cockroach to the ground. Giving him a nudge with her finger, she watches as he makes his exit, scurrying stage left. Ana applauds.

The guard says, "Come on, Dancer, you're on." He lifts her gently by the elbow, and together they begin their pas de deux.

# VODKA AND ICE
## *Charles Rutter*

An elderly blind man reclines on the lawn and pours a Blood Mary into his I.V. The Tabasco burn bites his arm until a pickle clogs the vein. He rolls his eyes in his hands and sighs as his grandson dresses beetles in formal attire.

"Whatcha doin?"

"Beetle wedding," the grandson says. "They've been living in sin."

The blind man feels his way to mixing a vodka drip and says, "Sometimes, kid, you have to ask yourself, 'Am I crazy, or is it the rest of the world?'"

The grandson switches a stag's loafers to a sextet of Florsheims. "It's you," he says, and measures a beetle for a tuxedo shirt.

The old man sets his eyes in the dirt to watch his back and adds tomato juice to vodka and glucose. "Either way," he says, "when you scream, there's the chance you'll find comfort in the echo."

# BEETLE
*Zach Andrews*

A beetle crossed the Place de l'Odéon.

Hello, he yells! And in my direction he takes the first unpredictable steps.

The Place is nearly empty. La Méditèrranée has settled between the lunch and dinner. The beetle is speaking to me. Two gumdrop cars whiz by and he waits for them to pass before crossing the street. These things make me nervous. He is a tremendously large *oryctes nasicornis*, which is a Rhinoceros beetle. As he walks up to me, he extends his arm, and we shake hands in front of the Odéon Theater. I had been sitting on the steps smoking a cigarette.

Hello, I said timidly. I always started to sweat in these situations. I felt comfortable around la femme de Ferdinand. She, too, was timid. She spoke very softly to everyone; she was unconfident, and insecure. I wanted her to be la femme de Richa-rd—la femme de Richie. I didn't think much of Ferdinand. It wasn't very fair. It wasn't fair at all, I thought.

Do you have another cigarette, the beetle asked?

Yes, I said. And I handed him one.

Thank you, he said politely. He was proper and polite. He stood tall, his shoulders back, head straight not tilted. However, I could still feel the blood hustling in and out of my chest. I always had this reaction when I met someone new.

Were you at the park, I asked?

No. But I thought about going.

It wasn't clear what would happen next. The beetle was quietly smoking. I anxiously waited and smoked the remainder of my cigarette. A full minute passed. The sound of motorbikes rose from the Boulevard Saint-Michel. The kids were out now. They are kids to me, I thought. I can't help thinking that.

So what is it that you're doing, the beetle asked?

Nothing really. I felt a kind of pressure to explain myself. I just like to sit here, I said. I was reading in the park.

That's good. It is a nice day, he reflected. I agreed, nodding my head. Well, said the beetle squarely, I need to get going. Do you think I could have another cigarette? I handed him one.

It occurred to me that I should be going as well. I had other things to do. And just then a gust of air blew warmly into the Place; I still had three cigarettes left, and I thought about staying.

Ok. I must be off, the beetle said. Perhaps I'll see you around. Thanks again for the smokes. Then he walked, a bit crookedly around the Place, and disappeared down the Rue de Vaugirard.

I sat back down on the steps of the theater. The wind brushed me again. I flipped open the pack of cigarettes—three left. I took one out and lit it. Sitting back on the steps of the Theater de l'Odéon, my body cooled against the shaded marble. I had been gone for a long time. It was harder to find pictures of people I knew back home. I want to be in love, I thought. The motorbikes screamed down the Boulevard.

# THE SOWER
## Jesse Goolsby

Five years ago Jennick beheld Van Gogh's *The Sower* in a textbook a couple months after his parents drowned in a violent storm on their way back from Stockholm. He remembers his eyes locking on page 178 of *European Art*. He cried while his teacher faced the chalkboard, so it lasted awhile, the circle of awareness spreading gradually until the entire class glanced toward the quiet giant, mouth agape, weeping into Van Gogh. And even now, when Jennick thinks about it, he is mostly alone—no siblings, no girlfriend—and yet he maintains a hope that something beautiful awaits him: a belief he's owed one from the universe.

4:48 PM

Jennick drives his bright yellow 1978 Cadillac Deville into the heart of Helsinki, already aware he'll be up all night. He huddles his seven-foot frame, knees bending high on each side of the gleaming steering wheel.

In this late afternoon Jennick excitedly imagines the possibility in the evening ahead. Two nearly completed cruise ships hulk in the shallows of the Baltic off to his left as he turns into the famous market square and parks the boxed boat of a car next to an early 80s Chevy Impala. No one knows how the old American car rallies started, but Jennick never misses one. He surveys the gaggle as Ari's black '69 Mustang pulls up, thundering out its gravelly song. The market square throbs with tourists wandering among pre-packaged flowers, watch peddlers, and seagulls that swoop down on children's ice cream cones.

"Enni's back from everything," Ari says. "She's calling me."

"Are you answering?"

Ari takes a couple hits from his cigarette.

"I'm answering," Ari says.

And then silence. Across the inlet sparks fly off of one of the cruise ships.

"I have a daydream where she shows up to my house grabbing her crotch. There's blood on her pants and blood on her hands and she shows me her hands. She wants to touch my dick."

"Jesus Christ, Ari."

"So I answer the damn phone."

6:57 PM

As Jennick and Ari drink vodka tonics at a bar off the market square, Enni comes up and hugs Ari around his neck. Ari doesn't look surprised.

"Is it bad to say I missed this?" Enni says, touching a freezing beer bottle to her forehead. When a table clears in the cramped bar they take it. Enni feels the poison in her drinks and her words slide into one another and her head leans to Ari's shoulder. She rubs his belly and laughs.

Jennick thinks about the world's fetuses and wonders why they die so quickly when removed. In an odd mental pulse he wonders if they drown in oxygen like fish. The connection to his parents isn't lost on him and for a moment he split-screens his vision: on one side, his parents scrambling, freezing, and slipping underneath the salt water, gulping heavy for a few seconds before the sink; on the other, a mini-human exposed to light and air, specks of lungs screaming for amniotic fluid.

10:12 PM

A sprinkle of rain arrives from the otherwise benign sky. Jennick can't feel his feet, and his limbs move lightly through the air. He smiles at everyone. He's lost Ari and Enni, and the streets have thinned; two women approach Jennick with the same late night sway.

"Basketball?" one of them asks. The answer is no, he doesn't play basketball, has never played basketball.

"Yep," he says, hoping, but the women bounce down the narrow street laughing.

He doesn't want to sober up, but the slight rain and basketball query thicken his blood.

Inside another bar, a stranger buys Jennick a drink, tells him about Andre the Giant, the famous wrestling entertainer of the 80s: how Samuel Beckett gave Andre rides to school, how Andre once chased four hooligans out of a bar and tipped the car over that they used as shelter, how the cops didn't believe their story: a giant chased you and tipped over your car?

"Can you tip over a car?" the man asks.

Soon thereafter, Jennick crouches behind the smallest car in the parking lot and lifts with all his hopeless might.

12:41 AM

Jennick shakes his head to clear the hallucination: the light rain and fire, the thin blue haze. Two more vodka tonics slosh through Jennick's massive body as he reaches high into the Finnish twilight, toward the flames and smoke that carve up apartments above him. A screaming bathrobed woman—infant in arms—leans far over a listing terrace railing. The people around Jennick dance and shutter and place their hands over their mouths. His vision strains to keep up. And then, Jennick sees the infant, a moment after the crazed mother balcony-drops her child into the fantastical air; the baby's disproportioned body slowly corkscrews downward at his outstretched arms five floors below. He wills his limbs to close in time, it seems so easy, but somehow they're late, and he feels the devastating smack of his empty arms.

3:22 AM

Jennick splays his long body on the steps of the white Helsinki Cathedral. He removes, then bundles his shirt at his lower back. He can hear music in the distance among the timeless night, the haunted dusk dawn of no-when. Jennick closes his eyes and pictures the sea regurgitating his parents. Then: *The Sower.* He focuses on the dark solitary figure, the cap, the bag, the right arm slinging seed out of the frame; it's all in shadow, and the seeds morph into fetuses mid-air; he sees the sower tossing them down into purple-gray fields that stretch into the never setting sun.

# PRELUDE TO A KISS
*Erik Morsink*

Whenever Henry tried to kiss her, Sara leaned towards him with pursed lips. He languished in expectation. His eyelids drooped.

She blew air into his face and drew away laughing, every time.

When he couldn't stand it anymore, he brought her to the wharf, and they boarded a ferry. Sara leaned over the railing with the men to watch the trucks backing up the landing ramp. When the ramp had been hauled up, she joined Henry on the upper deck to watch the port, the city of Milazzo, and the Sicilian coast recede and disappear.

Two hours later men threw lines from the ship onto the wharf of the island of Lipari. The ship's ropes were attached to the lines. Men standing on the wharf hauled them out of the water and slipped them over the mooring dogs. A man in an orange safety vest gestured for the landing ramp to be lowered onto the wharf.

Why would a man ask a woman where he can get a shave? Men seemed to like the question. The island's barber shops were located at the end of the wharf.

Henry opened one eye when he heard the sound of paper tearing, and he saw the barber put a fresh blade onto a cutthroat razor that looked exactly like a jackknife. Henry closed his eye. He heard the barber lathering up a brush.

The barber asked, "Where are you from?"

"I'm American."

Henry felt the stiff bristles of the brush hover over his upper lip.

"Mustache, too?"

"Yes."

The barber pressed the brush against Henry's left cheek, his right cheek, his chin, his neck. Suddenly the flourishes of the bristles stopped and the brush was gone.

The barber held the blade perpendicularly against Henry's right cheek and dragged it up toward the cheek bone. When the cheek was clean, he pressed the blade against the sideburn next to Henry's right ear and made a quick downward motion. Henry felt the blade under his nose, and then it slid down his lip. Sounds from the port came in through the open door.

When the face was beardless and wet, the barber covered it with foam again. This time, he took hold of the skin with the thumb and forefinger of his left hand and pulled it taut. He pulled the flesh under the ear toward the back of the head, and the blade slid up the cheek.

Another client entered the shop, sat near the door, and rustled the sports pages distractedly.

The barber pinched the right cheek gently, pulled it towards the right ear, and drew the blade down the taut upper lip.

The man sitting near the door said he was thinking about buying a piece of land and a house from another man. He told the barber that the asking price was too high.

The barber, between strokes of the blade, commented that it was a good piece of land. He admitted that the house was not perfect.

A stream of steaming water was absorbed by a cloth, which was then pressed against the face below the nose. The cloth was soaked again and pressed against the face. A dry cloth came next. Then the barber scooped some cream out of a jar with his fingertips and rubbed it in. He brushed Henry off and removed the smock.

"All right?"

"Great."

Back on the wharf, Henry found Sara with a newspaper and a cup of coffee at a table a few doors down. She wanted to know if the barber had made Henry puff up his cheeks one at a time to get a closer shave. She imitated the barber, "Puff air into your left cheek. Ok, now puff up your right cheek."

"No, he just pulled on the skin with his other hand."

"Your skin is so smooth."

They took a bus to the other side of the island and walked back. It was spring, and the island was green and dotted everywhere with the gold of lemons. They came down the old mule path into the city in the late afternoon and reached the port just as a ferry was mooring.

The cloud formations over the sea to the west made the sunset remarkable that evening. Sara saw it from a window in the salon where the truck drivers played cards on a tipped over waste-paper basket. Henry, whipped by the wind, saw it from the upper deck.

The next morning, they stayed in bed. Sara said, "Your face is still smooth."

Henry said, "The women of Lipari have fought long and hard to keep this local tradition alive."

Sara leaned towards him with pursed lips.

Henry's eyelids drooped. He languished in expectation. He already felt Sara's wet mouth on his own.

# BRIDGE PARTY
## *Bryan Jansing*

We're all lined up against a wall, stoned, drunk, with a nine millimeter and an uzi pointed at us—Christ, some things never change. I can't remember the last time we were all together like this. At least five years, maybe four. That's when we all still lived here, before college and the Navy, before careers and kids and divorces. Before we were even old enough to drink in America or even care. It had to be five years. But the last time we had a bridge party? Now that was quite a bit ago.

The carabinieri, the Italian military police, are talking to the black girl, Kathy, a sweetie of Skippy's. They think she's Moroccan and want to see her immigration papers. None of us are allowed to move, so we're pretty nervous, shivering mostly from the moist Veneto air that we are no longer accustomed to—at least that's our excuse.

They came from over the hill that hides the small country road. Above us runs the Milano-Venezia highway, hence the name, bridge party. But from down here, we couldn't hear them. Empty bottles litter the ground, a canal of the Po River separates us from the nearest house to the west and large fields separate us from anything else. This is where we used to come when we were all in high school. All the American kids, mostly military brats, were invited and because it was only a mile and a half from Skippy's place and my house, we often rode bikes. Coming over that dirt hill you would find at least one hundred drunk American teenagers and a bonfire nearing two stories high blazing, music blasting.

It must have been the couple in the little Fiat Panda, the one that we stormed in on when we first arrived. They must have been going at it, we didn't check. But it had to have been them. Jimmy, being Jimmy, almost hit them when he came over the dirt hill from the road. But, shit, he didn't hit them. Course, I can't imagine how disturbing it must have been for that guy, his girl mostly naked, them going at it and like the invasion of Sicily, we come roaring in on them, except we're drunk and belligerent.

"*Chi qui parla Italiano?*" the carabiniere with the uzi asks.

We all look at each other. None of us want to speak up. All of us speak Italian, except for the black girl who's struggling to explain that everything is all right and that she's not Moroccan.

"*Nessuno parla Italiano?* No one speaks Italiano?"

We don't answer. We're all too scared and we keep looking at one another. Mostly everyone is looking at me because they too recognize the carabiniere's roman accent. It's a roman thing, my mother is from Rome and my Italian is roman, therefore, the carabiniere with the uzi and I are of the same breed. But just when I'm about to speak, the other carabiniere barks at us.

"*Chi e', Skeeeppee?*"

We can't help it and burst out laughing. A row of six drunk Americans lined up against a highway pillar, laughing at a man with an uzi. Christ, I miss Italy.

The carabiniere with the nine mil seems to find us funny. Skippy finally musters up some courage and answers.

"*Io sono* Skippy."

"Do you know the Moroccan?" he asks in Italian.

"Yes, she's our friend."

"We received an anonymous phone call saying a group of men were raping a Moroccan girl."

What a relief. At the thought of Kathy being called '*marrochina*' we all laugh. The carabiniere with the nine mil looks at us suspiciously, while Skippy leaves us to talk to the other carabiniere.

"We're laughing because she's American," I say in my thickest roman accent.

"Ah, I understand." He reaches in his pocket and pulls out a cigarette, waving the gun around with the typical carelessness of the Italian authorities.

"May I light a cigarette?" Aldo asks in Italian.

"Of course."

At that, all six of us whip out cigarettes and light up.

I begin laughing to myself. It's all okay. Nobody's going to jail, we're in the clear. I'll be catching that flight to Colorado tomorrow.

After a few minutes Skippy walks back to us.

"The MP's are on their way," Skippy says.

"Stay here until the MP's show up. They want to

speak to you," says the carabiniere with the uzi. Then they turn and walk up the dirt hill.

As soon as they reach the top of the hill we all jump into our cars and bail. Dealing with the carabinieri is one thing, dealing with those numbskull Americans—now that's a different beast.

# IN MEXICO
*Teresa Milbrodt*

"A great hotel," he said. "Palm trees all around," he said. "Very romantic, and it's cheap."

The last part should have warned me, but it didn't. I pinched pennies and so did he, which explains how we first fell in love with each other's frugality, but I wasn't willing to be uncomfortable to save money. I swear all the palm trees outside were plastic and management pumped in cheap gladiola perfume from some unseen source. For breakfast we ate greasy tortillas and fried eggs, then he opened the sliding glass door to vent his cigarette smoke. He liked smoking in bed and I didn't let him do that at home, so it was his idea of vacation.

I shuffled to the outdoor market but along the way there were little kids with peso-wide eyes and for two seconds I was mad that my vacation had to be interrupted by the problems of the world, then I was mad at myself for being mad. At the market I bought mangoes and papayas then I stopped at a store for penny candy and gave it to the kids as I walked back to the hotel, their hands thin and needful. I imagined those fingers suddenly stiff. Cold. It was part of the bane of my profession, and why he said I was too morbid.

I walked into the hotel room and he was dozing and the comforter was smoking, three more seconds and it would have been synthetic flame. I didn't scream because there wasn't time, just grabbed the bucket of melted ice and threw it on the black spot and his shorts and he sat up with a "Shit" and saw the charred comforter. I dropped my bag of overripe fruit next to him. We sat on the edge of the wet bed.

"Sorry," he said.

"It's okay," I said, but I wanted to be home with the bodies I knew would be piling up. I wanted to wade through muscle and bone and confirm causes of death because that was useful. That gave people closure. The cause of his death will be smoking one way or the other. I used to smoke but the profession made me quit. When I got home at night I didn't tell him about dissecting black lungs. That was part of the politeness of love.

He wanted to smoke by the pool and the maid came into our room while I was eating a mango and I said we'd pay for the comforter but she didn't look disturbed by the burnt blanket, just got us a new one like this happened a lot, and maybe it did. I laid down for a nap on the clean comforter and the room smelled of smoke and so did my dreams. I dreamed of cutting him open, using delicate snips because I really did love the man, but I found his lungs were charred and his heart was light blue. In the dream I knew that meant he was willing, but I didn't know for what. His veins were filled with smoke and it puffed through his dead fingertips, but when those wisps dissipated I saw his fingers were curled, like the moment he died he was trying to grasp something he never touched.

# **LEADER OF MEN**
## *Meg Tuite*

He was a tall, good-looking man, though his features bore the slight tremor of the frenzied, similar to that strained purposefulness of a dog that has come to the end of its chain, but does not agree. He was waving a butcher knife out in front of himself while he spoke, and with each thrust, the knife, a bit of a yes-man itself, nodded up and down in obvious collusion with the man who held it, giving an added force to the man's words that alone they didn't carry. The woman watched the man and the knife equally, but said nothing, though her face, exquisite in its own right, said everything. They stood in front of a wounded tomato that the woman had been brutally mutilating before the man had been able to assess the seriousness of the situation and rush in to salvage it from its complete demise. There the tomato sat in front of them, bleeding to death from its right side, a savage testimony to the woman's complete and utter incompetence.

"Wrong," the man said. "Wrong, wrong, wrong!"

He snatched up the knife quickly, calling a halt to this obscene bloodbath. Was it necessary for him to be everywhere at once? Was there nothing that the woman wouldn't destroy if left to her own devices? She understood nothing—absolutely useless. The man held the knife forcefully, and with authority, letting it know immediately that he was in charge now, and it was to do exactly as he said.

"Look," he said. "Look at the knife. See how I hold it?" It was true. In his hand the knife was pointed and dangerous. It was a weapon, an extension of himself. The woman's reddened, shriveled hand had reduced the knife to nothing more than a feeble, clumsy thing that fumbled ridiculously with vegetables, pawing them into a slow and painful death. The blade stuttered and hung its head foolishly, until it became as dull and lifeless as her tongue.

The man looked over at the woman once more. His eyes rolled together in disgusted formation from one side of his head to the other, a trembling final summation of his entire contempt, and without another moment's hesitation he gripped the knife like nothing less than a leader of men, and using swift, competent, ruthless strokes, sliced the remaining portion of the tomato that the woman had not been able to deface, whereupon the tomato-eighths, also prepared to show her a lesson she would not soon forget, dropped neatly away from each other and lined themselves up efficiently, cleanly, and precisely—like well-trained little soldiers in uniform red. The man gave the woman one more derisive look and swaggered out of the kitchen. The woman stared at the tomato, and then after the man.

"This is your head," she said. She slammed the remains of the tomato against the wall and watched them slide artfully, gracefully down to the floor.

# BREAKFAST
*Lee Griffith*

"How do you like your eggs?"

Kirk sat up in bed. Molly stood topless in the center of the small studio apartment, between the foot of the bed and the stove, Kirk's skillet slung from her hip.

"Good morning," he said. "You sure are—"

He wanted to say *naked, you sure are naked*, but thought better of it. He didn't want to make Molly feel self-conscious. Self-consciousness was the enemy of toplessness. How he reacted right now could set the tone for the whole relationship. Their future sprawled out before Kirk in succeeding images of blissful meals: breakfasts *au naturel*, lunches in the altogether, dinners disrobed—maybe even snacks stark-naked, barbeque in the buff, and definitely an indecent Sunday brunch—he imagined every repast prepared and eaten in various stages of undress.

He removed his own shirt.

"Look at you," she said. "So sleepy. Like a

hibernating bear."

Molly rested the skillet on the edge of the foldout bed and inched across the sheets to kiss him. He worked his hands under her long black curls and kissed back, hard.

"Well, tell me. How do you like your eggs?"

She was still close, leaning into him, and one of her nipples touched Kirk's chest. He barely heard the question.

*Topless*, he thought. *I like my eggs served topless.*

"Kirk?"

"Fried," he said. Fried is good."

"Okay then."

Molly scooted off the bed and turned to the stove, placing the skillet on the burner. After she sliced butter into it, she turned around, scanning first the blankets, then the floor.

"What are you looking for?" Kirk asked.

"My blouse. I don't want to get burned by spattering grease."

Molly lifted the blankets and peered inside.

"Poached," he said.

"Excuse me?"

"Just poach my eggs. No grease." *No shirt*, he thought.

"Okay. But I still need a shirt, or I'll get scalded."

She kneeled on the linoleum to search under the bed.

*Scrambled?* he thought. No good. There'd still be hot butter. Hard-boiling was out of the question.

"Can you bake an egg for me?" Kirk asked.

"You want quiche?" Molly looked up from the floor.

"Yes." Kirk nearly sighed the answer, imagining

Molly's naked torso gyrating as she whipped an egg into submission.

"Fine, but I'm still putting on a top."

Her eyes landed on Kirk's t-shirt as he pushed it under the blanket.

"Give me that," she said.

"No."

"Come on. Give it to me."

Now it was ruined, Kirk thought. All ruined.

"Do you want breakfast?"

"If you make it topless."

Molly reached across Kirk and yanked the shirt from his hand. She pulled it over her head and returned to the stove. She scrambled an egg and ate it standing at the counter. The room smelled like butter and salt. Kirk imagined how plain the egg must taste.

# ANOTHER CHEESE RUN
*Mark Fallon*

And here you are again, boots unlaced, sockless, February, in the last aisle at 7-Eleven, hunkered and looking for Monterey Jack, same as you were last Tuesday and two nights the week before and you're telling yourself, fingering a brick of cheddar, that she'd better settle on the baby's name before he pops because these whimsical 2 AM cheese runs she's so fond of sending you on are really good at freezing your balls off and why can't it be July, or just a bit warmer—but it's not like you've *planned* this, not like she *deliberately* got knocked up, although there was still that night, that night, around the same number of months ago, when you were shitfaced on Ketel One and she took care of the condom, although you've stopped obsessing about that any longer—even though she won't admit it—because you love her, have actually loved her from the moment, on your third date, when, arriving late, you spied her through the window of that downtown sports bar, all shoulder blades and Rita Hayworth hair, looking furious and digging in her purse for what you felt, at the time, had there been any sense of poetry in the world, should be small black gun but turned out to be her cell phone, and having the unbearable joy of seeing every jealous jock turn, when she did, to check out the dude who had kept this woman waiting; so fuck your freezing balls, fuck that she may have done this or she may have done that, or even that when you get home she'll probably already be asleep. The last thing you'll be thinking is of names: Jon? or Peter? maybe David? or Tom? as she murmurs "thanks," and rolls away from you to the other side of the bed.

# WHERE'D THE CHEESE GO?
*Jason Sinclair Long*

None of them could remember why they started calling Grandpa "the cheese" in the first place.

But that was the last thing on their minds the night he disappeared.

Hours of panic, phone calls to friends, combing the neighborhood… nothing.

It was after midnight when he emerged from the attic burdened with newspaper clippings of the old days and cheeks full of tears.

# CHEESE
*Natania Rosenfeld*

In the tiny department store, I watched a man who hovered a long time over the cheeses. An excellent cheddar was on sale, in a fridge full of chunks all exactly the same size, but the man was pondering them as if it were necessary to pick the perfect chunk. The man's appearance was characterized by a jolly ordinariness. He was so ordinary I felt sure he must be a plainclothes policeman or guard making sure no one stole cheese. Why would he hover so long, yet appear so inconspicuous? Even his jolliness started to seem suspect as he turned over one large wedge of cheese after another. Strange. Worth watching, as long as he didn't take me for a criminal of some kind. Maybe he was a criminal himself, planning to hold up the deli section at an auspicious moment. I got a little scared and backed off, but curiosity took over again.

Finally, the man chose two cheeses and walked to the counter with one in each hand, like a ruffian about to throw stones, except that he held them with delicacy. He smiled at the cashier, who smiled at him, and he left with his two cheddars, looking pleased. This was too much for me; I had to follow. The man got on a bus not far from the department store, and I got on too, keeping a judicious distance between us. I took out the mystery I was reading, careful not to let the suspense get the better of me so I'd forget to check on the cheese man. He looked out the window, smiled at his fellow passengers, kept up the ordinary jollity aura so that those who noticed him seemed reassured by his presence—though most people didn't notice him. Exactly the sort of person you pass on the street and don't take a second look at, the sort of person who keeps us comfortable in our society by padding the edges and the middle, too, with his soft ordinariness. A beefy man, except his skin was too light to be beef; his skin was creamy. A corpse was discovered, the third, in quite a gruesome state, and I almost forgot to check on mister and glanced up just in time to see him pulling the Stop cord. At his stop, I got off too, keeping a few other people between us.

He became more and more charming as I followed him up several blocks. His walk had acquired a little lilt. See, I thought, this is what you discover if you trouble to look behind the façade of the ordinary. Here is this beefy man with his two cheeses, lilting. And here was I, creeping along at a distance, dressed in red and yellow which did not show to advantage, suddenly, against his grey-blue accountant/plainclothes policeman camouflage. I took care to keep just the right number of yards between us. He turned into a front walk, took out a key, disappeared inside a house before I was quite ready to react. Luckily, the front garden had a tree, climbable. In fact, the tree had a treehouse, and slats nailed to the trunk made it extremely easy to climb up and into a little haven in the leaves, a neat miniature house with heart shapes painted on the walls and the initials M.M. + N.N. chalked inside the biggest of the hearts. I settled into the treehouse in such a way that I could look out its front door without being seen myself, or so I hoped. Across from me was a second-floor window, and behind the window a bed, and a woman lying on it in underpants only, no bra. Her breasts and thighs were full, and she seemed pensive, anticipatory. The man walked into the room and she looked up in delight. He carried a plate in each hand, on each plate one of the chunks of cheese, and next to the cheese—if eyesight did not deceive—a knife, and tucked into the waist of his pants, a loaf of bread.

The man and woman received each other with cozy sighs of pleasure. He put the two plates on the bed, she gazed at them happily, and he took off his clothes except for his underwear. He was wearing the sort of boxers ordinary, middle-aged men wear, undistinguished except for a large pineapple on the bottom and apples and oranges in front. The woman delved hungrily into her chunk of cheese with her knife and ripped a hunk off the proffered loaf. More delicately, he took a slice from his own cheddar, then sliced himself a piece of the bread. Two styles. They ate with equal gusto, at first just chewing, making pleasurable faces, savoring. Then they began to talk to each other between bites. I could see their mouths moving, their expressions fully alive. Once, his hand reached out and brushed a crumb from her breast; it fell onto her thigh, and he wet a fingertip, picked the crumb up and inserted it in his mouth. This was a moment of such obvious communion that they stopped chewing and beamed at each other.

After some time, the woman came to the window. Her breasts looked at me like eyes, the areolas irises, the nipples pupils. Her navel was a mouth. She gazed at the treehouse for a long moment, intent, then lowered the blind. I sat on in the little hut for hours, seeing nothing, hearing nothing, my vision blurred, my body strangely paralyzed. It was nightfall when I climbed down at last, cramped, needing to straighten but unable to, retracing steps to the bus stop with a crabbed gait.

# LIGHTNING WATCH
*Dustin M. Hoffman*

Carrie and I watch the best storm of July from the balcony of our apartment. Drops pelt our scalps, puddle in the sagging seats of lawn chairs. The sprinklers in the courtyard rattle, *shut, shut, shut*. A violet Y strikes close, but Carrie's eyes are diverted, lower—third floor balcony across the courtyard. She points with the neck of her beer. Backlit by yellow kitchen light, silhouettes of neighbors embrace, reach into shadows, touch cheekbones, pull up each other's shirts. Lightning loses its mystery a little. Now the flash reveals a flicker of flesh. We can't look away, and feel hidden with our lights off, our bodies still in darkness. Between thunder cracks and gutter pour, I hear laughter. I can't tell if they are inside the screen slider or out. Do they feel rain on their skin? Did they come to watch the storm too, but were impassioned by weather? Are his fingers calloused like mine? Do they know that we watch? An indigo X darts through my peripherals. Under my eyelid, where it is black, the lightning is a shrinking red cross. Now I have X and Y, the faded equation of July. Who could form a solution from this? The neighbors stumble into the kitchen, flooded for a moment in light bulb glow revealing bra straps fallen from shoulders and denim slipping from waists. The light goes out. There is nothing under my eyelids, but Carrie touches my hand. We go inside and close the blinds.

# THE STORM
*Curtis Smith*

The siren sent the children scattering to the hallway. They sat as they'd been taught—knees up, bowed heads covered by their hands. The lights flickered and died. In the darkness, a boy cried for his mother. The window at the hallway's end looked out on a purple sky. Lightning cracked. Playground mulch pelted the window, a few specks at first, then steadier, harder. Another flash, and the sizzle of split air was felt on their necks and hands. The wind shrieked, and the pitch escalated until it swallowed the teacher's screams for everyone to stay down. Through the window, they watched the roof of the custodian's shed lift and tumble across the kickball field.

Denny, the large boy from the special class at the end of the hallway, rose to his feet. He shook off the teachers who tried to make him sit. He was like that, mute for the most part, content in his cut-off world until he exploded in fists and tears. Denny sucked a high-diver's breath and screamed. To the children, he was no more than a silhouette, a figure just a shade darker than the window's midday black. His wail swelled, a coiling that rose from his ribcage and gut, a cry culled from a reservoir of fear the others were only now understanding. The boy howled until he dropped, gasping, to his knees. The hallway window shattered, and in the next second, outside and in changed places.

# MARGE
*Devin Murphy*

When Marge beat the shit out her drunken husband, Robby, in the middle of our courtyard, she changed the way I viewed things forever. Marge was pushing three hundred pounds that she carried mostly in her Frisbee sized eyeballs. Her stare froze children long enough for her to scoop them up in her warm banister arms and croon to them like the Salamanca River was flowing from her mouth. We could always hear her singing until Robby rolled in yelling and screaming about how ugly she was. Then everyone in our row would alternatively laugh or cringe.

Robby was lengthy as a twisted up bed sheet in the wind, and he let his graying blond hair grow out of his mesh Buffalo Bills hat like a scarecrow. He was a car mechanic who would stumble off the bus every night cussing his way to his trailer where he'd start wailing on his wife. My mom and some of the other ladies would always yell at him to, "Take it easy," or

"Don't go doing nothing mean," but that's what he was all about, and for as long as I remember, Robby was always up to something mean.

We'd all seen him haul off and take big swings at her, thudding his fists against her flanks and the side of her head. There was always a roar of women's voices screeching at him if this was going on in the quad. The women's voices had so much fear, hate, and hurt in them it was as if their yelling was an instinctual call for their own safety.

So when I heard the women start yelling one day I wasn't surprised. But when my mom called me, "Dedee, come here, baby," I could tell in her voice something was happening and I went to our stoop. The whole row was quiet, but everyone was watching.

Marge had cutoff jean shorts on and was hunkered forward, jumping up and down like the older boys do when they get in fights. Her purple t-shirt was swaying all over her body. Robby was pushing himself off the ground. When he stood up his legs were all watery. He lifted his misshapen head of hair and Marge punched him in the face as hard as I'd ever seen anyone get punched. Robby dropped like he'd been melted. He bounced up slurring his words. Marge collared him by the back of his dull blue mechanic's shirt and started tossing him around the quad. His limp legs slapped around in the air and slammed to the ground. Each time he got up he tried punching Marge, who was moving so quick I think we were all stunned.

"Bitch," "Filthy Cow," and every other nasty thing you can imagine saying to a person was getting squeezed from Robby's mouth as she jumped on top of him and started clubbing her fist onto his head.

Marge's voice was booming over him and taunting him with questions, which was how people fought here, always yelling, "You think you can whip my ass?" or "You didn't think I'd hurt you, did ya, did ya?" So Marge yelling, "You just gonna shack up with me cause you can't do no better," sounded like a question to me. She went on, yelling and asking with each shot she landed, "You just gonna use me up?"

Finally, some of the older boys came and dragged Robby off so Marge wouldn't kill him.

I asked Mom what happened.

"Robby said he didn't want no fat babies," Mom told me.

I couldn't figure out the details, but I knew Robby and Marge had some agreement that he'd just reneged on and it made me feel like I'd just been punched in the gut, too. After that fight I stood by my mother as she walked the row talking to the rest of the people in the complex the way we did after every big event. We went from stoop to stoop and each place seemed a lot more complicated than it had before. All of a sudden I saw that there was some pact, or version of a pact, or the aftermath of such pacts in each of these trailers I'd grown up around.

It made me wonder where my father was, and if my mom was lonely without him, and how lonely Marge would be without anyone. It made sense to me why she'd snapped. I felt like it was justified too, as if we'd all had something immense taken away from us when Robby told her he didn't want no fat babies, like after he said that, and after he'd been beaten and dragged off and everything got quiet, there was no covering we were all living according to those random agreements, and none of us fully controlled the terms.

# **HERE IN THIS**
*Faye Kicknosway*

He lived longer than her, and her mad as hell he did it. He lived louder and louder, never mind what she'd say about it. Never mind her spindly voice wheedling up at him from her chair, from the stick lifting clothes to the wringer from one wash tub to the other, and from it to the basket, and the clothesline in the back yard. He was alive and could tamp her voice down with a trowel if it tried to snake its way up a weed, or drown it with the garden hose, or flush it down the toilet, or bury it in the trash the garbage man took away.

He was alive and she was the one had skinny death blowing his cigar smoke up her nose as worms picked their teeth with what fell from his chin. Not her plan at all, him full throttle alive, belching loud enough to call fire trucks to the front door, his fingers twiddling at his nose and crotch, farts lining up to warm the seat of his pants: the hippo fart; the mouse fart; the kangaroo; the owl; the whale's fart; the dog's as it rolls in the mud, as it sleeps beside the bed.

He was alive longer than she'd have allowed it if she'd had a say in it. He grinned at his strudel, at the noises around him, newspapers shook open and folded, the weight of shoulders pushed down into elbows and forearms, men hunched over their plates, levering table legs into the floor.

Cold air slapped at the heat in the room when the door opened, hatted men in butcher's aprons coming in, steam rising from their coats as they took their gloves off, stuffed them into their pockets, grabbed trays, napkins caged around a fork, spoon, knife, and stood in line behind other men, looking thoughtfully at the food spread out for them to choose from. Outside a voice yelled God at cars trawling for a parking place, it picked up and mimicked by men hog-carrying burlap sacks, or pushing holes through the crowds with forklifts loaded with crates and boxes and bails to re-stock stalls set up since one in the morning.

"You eat like that, I'll have to bury you in a shipping crate because no coffin'll be big enough to hold you," she'd said. "And I'll have to hire a crane to drop you in a hole dug big enough to hold it. That means both our plots; and where will my final rest be?"

There were six pats of butter and a heel of black sour dough Russian rye bread on a plate, and steak and three eggs and hash browns, and coffee enough to ballast both his legs until he got home and made a pot.

"Contrary's what you are," she'd said, and complained to her girlfriends about him. "He's hardly ever home. I never know where he is or when he'll be back. And he's eating himself into his grave and there's nothing I can do about it. I can't watch him every minute, and it wears me out, scolding at him all the time."

He leaned back in his chair, fork in his hand, eyes closed, listening to the coughs and wheezes, the nose blowing, the hiccups, the burps and belches, the laughter in all its shapes: whistling down a nose; eddying up the throat from the belly, the chest; chortled; guffawed; whinnied; trilled; chuckled; laughter that came in spasms and gasps, made the eyes run with tears, and the hand pound the table or wipe the nose or point the fork at the man across the table, what he'd said, and men repeating it to other men who leaned in to hear.

"You'll probably die right here, your head in your plate, and a stranger will call the cops and you'll wind up in the morgue, and get cut open and all the junk you eat will spill everywhere and they'll blame *me*, it's my fault, *I* did it to you; it was *me*, and not your bad habits that killed you. *No*, you're *not* going to do that to me. From now on we'll do our shopping, put it in the car, and go right home where I'll make us a good, healthy meal."

He sopped bread in the egg yoke on his plate, lifted it to his lips, some of it dribbling down his whiskered chin to his sweater. He wiped at his chin with his hand, then smeared it across his sweater, broadening the stain on it, picked his scarf up from the chair next to him, and wiped his hand on it.

# DEAD AND ALIVE
## *Michael Spring*

He had cancer. It was terminal. The doctors said he had weeks to live. Richard still didn't understand why he chose now to write love notes to Nancy, who was Richard's wife.

Nancy showed them to Richard when she came off duty. She was a nurse at the hospital.

At first, the notes had been unsigned and sporadic. Now, with death hovering close over him, he had become brazen.

"I long to drown in your silken hair, to trace the line of your moist lips with my finger, to have you sigh in my arms." The spidery writing straggled across the scented page.

"Does he write these things himself?" Richard asked.

"He would hardly dictate them to his wife," Nancy said. "She's his only visitor." His wife sat with him for hours.

Richard suggested increasing his pain relief.

"Nothing fatal. Just something to reduce him to a coma."

Nancy disagreed. "This fantasy is keeping him alive," she told him.

She didn't tell Richard that she was writing back.

"I can almost feel your hot breath on my body," she wrote, confident in the knowledge that he would be dead in days.

Instead, one of the nurses found that he had limped to the toilet with a copy of *Playboy* magazine.

Slowly, the colour returned to his skin.

The notes continued. "When we awake in darkness, I will taste your hungry lips, and you…"

She wanted to encourage his recovery. She wore more makeup than normal. She found excuses to visit his room, to wipe his brow, straighten his sheets. Sometimes, as she stretched across him, her breast grazed his forehead.

She wondered how he would look if he recovered. She imagined him tanned and healthy, on an exercise bicycle in the gym.

But the next morning when she entered his room, she found his wife leaning over him with a pillow. They looked at each other without comment. The monitor was flat-lining, making its dull, lifeless warning sound.

Nancy couldn't help but notice, as she pressed the button, which would alert the recovery team, that one of her notes was on the floor beneath the bed.

**OBLIVIOUS TO THE INCREASINGLY HARMFUL EFFECTS OF EACH OTHER'S EXPONENTIAL REGRETS ON THE RELATIONSHIP, THEY KEPT ON SQUEEZING SOFT WHITE REASONS FROM THE EVERYDAY PORN OF A HUNDRED THOUSAND DISTANT POSSIBILITIES MISSED**

*Travis Macdonald*

Which was nice so they decided to do it again next Wednesday.

# THE THINGS WE TAKE AND THE THINGS WE LEAVE BEHIND
*Ashley Cowger*

His boxes are skimpy and there are only three of them, each labeled with a number that corresponds to a detailed list in his wallet—handwritten as he filled each box and then typed after each item had been carefully categorized and alphabetized. My boxes are overstuffed, bowing out at their cardboard walls and overflowing at their tops, and there are far too many of them. Many more than three, which was the number we agreed on two months ago.

He says I am materialistic.

I say he is heartless.

Because you'd have to be to get rid of the pocket watch that your grandfather gave you, the one that his grandfather gave to him and his grandfather gave to him. Or to donate to charity the afghan that your mother gave to *both of us* as a wedding present, which she designed and knitted herself. Or to throw away the card that your coworkers were willing to spend a few uncomfortable minutes staring down at, agonizing over what awkward thing to say, like signing a high school yearbook: "Good luck." "Keep in touch." "It's been great knowing you."

I wonder what says more about you: the things you keep or the things you throw away.

Me, I've gone through my stuff. I told him I've gone through all of it countless times. I *can't* get rid of any more. This is my history. This is who I am. If we don't have our pasts then we have nothing at all.

My favorite childhood stuffed animal: a gorilla, worn threadbare now and with scratches covering her once black eyes. Every birthday card my grandparents ever sent me, including the two years in a row where they thought I turned ten, neither of which I did. The collar that my cocker spaniel used to wear before he got cancer and had to be put down, and especially the little heart shaped tag hanging from the collar with his name and mine engraved on it together.

He says I have to go through my stuff again. "You can't bring more than three," he says, and he's firm on this point, resolute with arms folded.

Obligingly, I get down on my knees and start sifting through my life again, even though I know already that I won't find anything else I can part with, just like I didn't the last time I looked through and the time before that. But life is all about compromise, so I empty each box item by item, and lay everything side by side on the floor and pick them up and inspect them one by one, just so he will know I'm doing all I can.

My collection of Lobster Pals, almost complete, only missing Papa Lobster, who one winter was the most sought after Christmas gift. My *World's Most Loved Children's Poetry* book, with pages wrinkled and brown from the time I dropped it into a muddy pond. My first pair of lace-up shoes, which, according to family legend, I spent almost three full hours tying and retying when I got them, committing to memory how to do it. My little league uniform, which was in fact the whole reason I joined the team—because I wanted to wear what *those kids* were wearing.

I can't throw these things out. I can't give them away. They are part of me, or I am part of them, or we are irreversibly entangled with each other. At least we once were. And sometimes late at night, when the noise of the TV and the hum of the refrigerator aren't enough to drown out the sound of nothing, I like to believe that we still are. That I am still that little girl who assigned meaning to inanimate objects, who saved these things because she believed that they mattered.

To get rid of these things would be too much of giving in. Compromise: a synonym for defeat. So I shake my head and I tell him again, "I'm keeping them." And before he can protest I begin scooping everything back into the boxes, which I proceed to tape shut and paste address labels on and then attempt to lift but can't.

He watches me, a look on his face that I can't quite read. We haven't been married long enough for that. A sort of half smile, half-taught lipped expression. His head is cocked to one side and his arms are still folded in front of him. He lets me struggle with a box for a second and when he steps forward I'm not sure if he's going to rip open the tape and dump the contents of the box on the floor or if he's going to lift it for me.

He does the latter and wordlessly carries it out to the car. When he comes back I'm not sure whether I should say, "Thank you" or whether I should still be angry, that he's doing it grudgingly, I guess, or that he thinks he has the right to tell me who to be. I decide on both.

Instead of saying, "You're welcome," he thanks me for thanking him and then surprises me by adding, "I guess if they mean that much to you…" He trails off before finishing the sentence but I know this is his sort of compromise.

"Thank you," I say again, and don't add that they don't mean "that much" to me, not exactly. It's just that I want them to. I want to believe that things sometimes matter. I want to believe that what we had when we were children we can still have when we grow older. That there are some things in life that are worth holding on to.

# THIRD STREET
*April Johnston*

He drove slowly, softly, easing the car over humps in the brick street. For once, the radio was off and all we could hear was the wind blowing new rain out of the trees and onto the windshield.

"Use your wipers," I whispered.

"They squeak," he whispered back. "I don't want to make any noise."

I smiled at him and slid my hand over my belly, where she used to live. He didn't care about noise then. Did we think she couldn't hear from inside of me? I couldn't remember what we thought. The two days since she'd appeared, all angry wails and fists balled into tight wads, felt longer than all of the days we'd waited for her. Longer than all of the days we'd spent chasing dust and dog hair out of the corners and crevices so the house would be perfect for her.

He parked the car on Third Street, under the flickering street lamp, and we twisted in our seats. She was asleep, her nearly bald head tipped to the side, her tiny lips parted in the middle. He reached over the headrest and slid the back of his finger down her arm.

"We're home," he whispered.

# THE KNIFE
## *Robin Hillard*

The children had gone with their father and as I sat by myself in the mall, blinking back self-pitying tears, a small boy put his hand in mine.

"Where's your mummy?"

He did not answer and a couple of teenagers giggled as they walked past.

I could not leave the boy by himself so I took him to the manager's office, where a fat man in a crumpled shirt was watching the cricket. When I told him about the boy he grudgingly turned away from the screen. "So where's the kid?"

The child was gone.

"Must have run back to his Mum," he said.

I was in the car, edging into the traffic when something snuffled beside me. The boy. Safely secured in the front seat belt.

I could not stop in the middle of the road. "I'll have to take you home," I said.

I'd give him a meal before I rang the police. And

if his mother did not come for him, I could take him to work.

Ted claimed our children for the holidays because, as he told the judge, a dress shop is no place for a child. But this boy was no trouble and Olinda, the manager, did not object to him. When we arrived, she muttered a few distracted words and darted off to serve a customer.

He was happy to play in the corner and, at lunchtime, I let him ride in the spaceship in the mall. A woman stared when I put in a coin.

On Sunday morning I still had the boy. What was his name?

Simon, I decided suddenly. He would be Simon. Until I found his family, I reminded myself.

I was not lonely with Simon in the house. He liked to sit on the kitchen bench, watching me cook, but he did not eat very much. He left most of his dinner on his plate.

After the holidays, when Sonny and Ursula came home, they hardly noticed the boy, as they chatted about their summer.

"Dad's getting another horse for us," Ursula said.

"I'm training to be a jockey." Sonny announced.

I set four places for dinner.

"What's that?" Sonny pointed to Simon's plate but, before I could reply, Ursula turned on the T.V. and they took their food into the sitting room.

Later, Simon trotted off to bed. My two whined for extra time and because it was their first day home I let them stay up late.

Tomorrow I would drive them to school. Shouldn't Simon be going to school with them? No need to worry about that, I told myself. He's not my child.

We settled into the term routine. Simon still did not talk to me but sometimes, from the kitchen, I thought I heard three voices chattering.

Of course children fight. Sonny and Ursula argued all the time, but Simon, the smallest, did not get involved.

'Til Ursula reached for a biscuit on his plate. A chocolate biscuit. He grabbed a knife. I snatched it away. Was that blood on the blade?

Simon scuttled out of the room; I followed, and stayed with him 'til he calmed down.

In the sitting room, Sonny was sitting quietly with Ursula and they were both shivering.

Things were more difficult after the fight. Simon resented my children and he was stronger than he looked. Sonny and Ursula often had bruises though I tried to keep them out of the visitor's way.

A teacher came from the school, with a young policeman. I told them all about Simon and, although it tore my heart, asked them to take the boy away.

But Simon did not go with the policeman. Sonny and Ursula went in the police car and Simon stayed with me.

# CATASTROPHE
## *Robin Hillard*

The shop had been closed for an hour but I sat at my cluttered desk, waiting for Edgar. A wardrobe was carefully placed to shelter my workspace from daytime customers; in the light of a small lamp its mirror scowled with my reflected face.

Edgar always sent his stuff at night, and while I was helping his men unload the van he would be at my house with my wife.

"Don't ask so many questions," he said, when I wanted to know why this night-delivered stock was only shown to favored customers. We needed the money so I held my tongue and the word *pimp* hovered between us.

My wife did not know Ramona was part of the deal.

"This one will make a man of you," Edgar said when he introduced the girl. He called her "payment in kind" and laughed. He thought I did not get the joke.

I would like to share the insult with my wife: *Your lover gave me a prostitute to pay for you!*

But tonight Edgar was driving the van himself and Isobel would have to sleep alone.

Thump. The wardrobe swayed as the cat jumped down.

"Catastrophe!" My wife chose the name because as it climbed around the shelves it often knocked our stock on to the floor, "That animal's a right catastrophe," she said, sweeping up bits of broken vase. "As useless as your shop."

That was before the night deliveries.

I'd have to find a way to wedge the wardrobe firm, or one day it would fall and flatten a customer. A real catastrophe.

Why was Edgar coming tonight?

"He probably wants to sell his grandmother's teeth," I told the cat as I poured kitty chow into its dish. It was too busy munching to respond but Edgar, coming behind me, laughed.

"What's an antique shop without a cat—eh puss?"

He reached to rub the ginger head but Catastrophe thought the man was after his food. There was a flash of claw, an oath and a kick.

"Bloody stray. Should be put down."

The sudden ill temper passed as he opened his case and pulled out a small plastic envelope. "I'm into something new. There's real money here."

"No way." I was not into drugs

"I think you are. And I've got something else." He waved a photograph.

"No drugs." I said it again.

"No?" There was a menace in his salesman's voice.

He put the picture face up on the desk: two bodies tangled on an antique bed. Ramona looked very young.

"Jail bait. She's just fifteen," he laughed. "So you'd better do what you're told."

He turned a contemptuous back as he piled more packets onto the desk.

Catastrophe crunched the last piece of kitty chow and climbed clumsily up the wardrobe. A sudden picture in my mind—a body jammed under the wood.

As Edgar straightened, I gave the wardrobe a push. It fell.

A splatter of blood. Was Edgar still alive? I banged his head with a heavy drawer to be sure he was dead.

*It was a burglar. I was having a smoke outside and heard the crash.* I looked at the mess on the floor and from broken shards of mirror-glass, my face grinned back.

The cat was rubbing itself against my leg as I prepared my voice to ring the police. *Catastrophe was true to his name*, I would tell my wife.

# **FORTY**
## *Michael Dean Clark*

### One
The gray-furred gift kitten from PetSmart claws her just under the right eye and the scratch immediately puffs into a red ridge that arches like a single-colored rainbow.

### Two
He offers but cannot pay for her visit to urgent care.

### Three
The doctor checks her just-becoming-plump twenty-eight-year-old upper body for bruises and she laughs to show she knows what he's looking for and he needn't worry with this guy.

### Four
In a limp whine she hasn't heard him use before, he apologizes thirty seven times on the bus ride home, none of which she asks for or expects.

### Five
They stop for drinks at the Applebee's on the same block as her cream-colored brick apartment

building and he insists on holding his cold-sweating pint glass against her cheek.

### Six
The skinny brunette waitress, with acne makeup can't cover riding both cheekbones, sighs and "ohs" and winks when she sees him pressing his drink against the gouge.

### Seven
She asks to go as soon as the waitress leaves, smiling without teeth and refusing to explain why she won't let him pay the bill.

### Eight
The three flights of stairs to her landing are silent except his heavy steps and her breath through a twice-broken nose.

### Nine
"Where's the cat?" he asks in her living room and she realizes it has no name.

### Ten
He wants to find Harriet—the name she chooses so they'll stop calling it "it"—but she imagines the hero pose that will come later and won't let him go alone.

### Eleven
She reaches out to knock on Mrs. Sarducci's door but he stops her, pointing to the gaping window at the end of the hall leading out onto the fire escape.

### Twelve
"Let's go back," she says, watching sloppy-fat raindrops splatter against the rusted metal window frame with a frown he'd call ugly-making.

### Thirteen
When they reach the roof six floors above she is soaked, angry, and decidedly opposed to the manic pinging of the rain slapping against the crumbling fire escape they've just climbed.

### Fourteen
"You check the ledges; I'll look in the middle," he says, his green eyes and girlishly small feet already moving away.

### Fifteen
She traces the rooftop's perimeter only partly paying attention while the scratch under her eye grows longer and deeper, throbbing in rhythm to the song in her head.

### Sixteen
Lightning flashes and she stops dead, feeling conspicuous against the near naked rooftop.

### Seventeen
Thirty feet away he notices Harriet huddled against an aluminum heat exhaust vent, her gray fur slick-soaked to her skin and yellow eyes furious.

### Eighteen
As he draws back his hand, he decides the scratch on his wrist is worse than the one under her eye.

### Nineteen
He relaxes for the first time all night.

### Twenty
She's next to him before he knows it and he thinks that with the way her wet brown hair mats against her small, annoyed face, she looks a lot like Harriet.

### Twenty One
"I tried to pick her up," he says, holding up his bleeding right wrist as evidence.

### Twenty Two
Unmoved, she thinks only that there was no rain to wash the blood from under her eye.

### Twenty Three
"I'll get her," she says, stepping around him.

### Twenty Four
Harriet bolts before she even reaches out, skitting between her legs, across the graveled roof, onto the

ledge, and over the side.
### Twenty Five
He runs to where it jumped, leaning over and scanning the sidewalk nine stories below while she trudges back to the fire escape.
### Twenty Six
"There's no way a cat just jumps off the roof like that," he says from the sofa, a tattered brown bath towel on his balding head while his old blue jeans leak into older orange cushions.
### Twenty Seven
"Harriet did."
### Twenty Eight
He sees she's happier without the cat and his laugh sucks the air from the room like a vacuum.
### Twenty Nine
He gets to the street before he realizes she did nothing at all to stop him from leaving, stared silently past him with dead brown eyes, didn't even move as he passed.
### Thirty
It's ten minutes to the kitchen closing at Applebee's when he slides into a booth, his damp jeans skidding across the red vinyl surface like a stutter.
### Thirty One
The waitress from earlier comes to his table and he smiles widely at her.
### Thirty Two
She takes his order—Guinness and a shot of "anything with a kick"—and leaves with no sign she remembers him, deciding she's too thin and not as cute as he thought.
### Thirty Three
In the apartment's bathroom with its peeling tan green wallpaper her thin pink lips curl around "Harriet" like a curse, and she studies the already

infected welt under her eye as if she'll see the spreading bacteria if she just looks closely enough.

## Thirty Four

She leaves a thick white smear of cortisone cream in the cut and walks back into the kitchen where she fills a pink-tinted sandwich bag with ice that's all corners, wraps it in a dish towel, and presses the cold to her cheek.

## Thirty Five

The eleven o'clock news is a rerun.

## Thirty Six

He calls three minutes after midnight, drunk and apologetic and mumbling about how impossible it is to find good help in a restaurant.

## Thirty Seven

His knock comes six minutes after they hang up and she sits motionless on the couch, the breath whistling through her fist-deviated septum.

## Thirty Eight

He only knocks twice and neither says a word.

## Thirty Nine

The door is unlocked, but he's not the kind of guy who'd check.

## Forty

The note he slips under the door is on the back of his Applebee's tab and she can't get past the "Suzy" with a smiley face in ball-point blue on the front.

# THINGS I SHOULD HAVE TOLD HER BEFORE SHE LEFT

*Ray Morrison*

1. Despite what you say, hating tomatoes is not a character flaw. It's a taste preference.

2. I am *not* the only one who cares about how much shoes cost.

3. Your mother is frequently full of shit. Perhaps always.

4. Whenever I'd leave the toilet seat up, I admit it was due to carelessness on my part. Except near the end, when I'd do it on purpose. Sometimes even when I didn't need to pee.

5. Your best friend Jan offered to blow me at your fancypants Christmas party last year.

6. Speaking of Jan, on some of those Friday nights that you and she had your "Girls' Night Out," she would call the house looking for you.

7. Oh…and after that happened a couple times,

I followed you; and unless Jan has magically grown to six-foot-two and grown a goatee, I think you were lying to me.

8. You should never, ever kiss a man who is not your husband in a motel parking lot.

9. Did I ever mention that I bought an expensive digital camera? Or that it cost about the same as three pairs of shoes?

10. Maybe it was my lawyer that I told about the camera.

11. By the way, "'til death us do part" is a vow, not a suggestion.

12. Vows are sacred and should be treated as such. I take vows very seriously.

13. I vow you'll never see a dime.

14. I don't know how she does it, but somehow Jan makes tomatoes taste great.

# THE WHISPER IN THE CHURCH, FLICKER OF THE CANDLE THERE
*Chris Bowen*

    They attended worship on Sundays worshiping and worshiping and worshiping for the day to come.
    "To love thy neighbor," the pastor said looking into eyes of the pair for a response to this and they would talk in counseling but never really blinking at any one given time.
    There was no regret to this when requesting the usual breakfasts with family and friends (Christian or not) to be put on hold or taking rain checks this Sunday seeming like every Sunday on towards a future of a dozen or so pieces of paper stabbed on the apartment desk with bills to get to sometime at the end of a lifetime, maybe the day after the wedding, maybe.
    The day was wide as a sun from people standing on a mountain or buried in a sea, though really right

now standing outside in line, it being so wide and recognizable that it stops moving so many things: gravity and laws are broken, hearts and jaws are broken, and cameras click far faster than the speed of light.

The crowd curled like fingers, enveloping towards what gaping rift an aisle and no random destination. Using the attention, each couple passing through bony but strong fingers of tradition here, breaking rank flawlessly at the second to third last step before the altar dividing attendees like what happens when you split an atom: ruckus.

Ruckus happens if you split an atom.

The violinist sits, bends and twists in retaliation to bring them back together as a whole (like any soldier) and in her efforts plays nothing but background music. But she is paid well and it continues and continues for so long until it sinks, sinking and sunk sending steps down a maid who hands flowers to a mother and on out the door, a stomach churning like batter relentlessly for that mother who realizes that batter must be baked, her hair all in a bun.

The violinist isn't paid well enough to stretch another note from bow to string and then does some wind whip the whisper in the church to begin and the flicker of the candle there, for something has split that has nothing to do with science.

# THE SIXTH QUEEN, CATHERINE PARR

*Sophie Rosenblum*

The con man is late for dinner, and I hardly notice because it's June and sunshine's still pouring through my windows like it's 7AM. Earlier, I found some stones, red jasper I kept as a kid for good luck. I put them in my pocket for me. The con man is balding and the bit of frizz on the top of his head holds three beads of sweat. "What's for dinner?" he asks, and sits hard in my mother's rocker.

I am his sixth wife. Three of the others are dead. Two are missing. I think about what I can offer. Or sometimes I think about when I will go. What will provoke him or bore him enough. We don't talk about the past. I make veal piccata, sometimes chicken, and he says, "What's tomorrow bringing?" and it excites me because I don't know.

# THE BATHTUB
*Brian Seeman*

In the bathroom, the water approaches the tipping point inside the tub, the waves rolling towards the edge and splashing beyond the realm of white porcelain onto a tile floor unprotected and soon to be sopping wet. With each instrument of his career plunging into the scalding water, the levels grow higher, the levee approaches uselessness, and the noises from the rest of the house drown away from Tonya.

Petri dishes are already floating. As are microscope slides, a Bunsen burner, and a handful of test tubes. They dip in and out, below and above the waves. Water streams from the spigot, the steam suspended in the air. Hands empty, she reaches for the bottle of shampoo. His brand, an off-brand. The type not to offer the care and detail of her brand, a kind promising long-lasting vitality and bounce. Life. Verve. Vivacity.

Cap open and upside down, the bottle splurges its

contents into the swirling bath, and Tonya presses her fingers into the plastic, summoning the fluid to do as it promises. Clean, cleanse, and most of all, relieve. Each drop of turquoise touches the surface, cresting the waves and creeping atop the instruments of her husband's life. A dab of the dandruff-eliminating product lands in a Petri dish, resembling one of the creations Greg has created. A culture, a bacteria, a lump of love. She drops the bottle and exits the bathroom, running down the hallway and back into the room he's called his lab.

The room is small but large enough that Greg had thought the world might be created within a smaller world, a lovelier world. There, in front of Tonya, sits the last thing left to be sunk, the one thing Greg considers his view into the new world, the one he's promised would flip their current world upside down and right-side up.

Tonya grips the microscope and starts back to the bathroom, where she can hear the water bubbling beyond the tub, breaking the levee and spreading across the floor. She is almost there when she passes the bedroom, and there, by the bed, the place where they once laid and loved, is Greg, licking lips and pulling pages from her family Bible, the good book with each of their good names inscribed on the inside.

Just as she's hated his way of life, he too has hated hers.

Torn pages float below, and with each one landing on the mattress, he reaches over and forces them to the floor, shouting, "This is fiction!"

She lifts the microscope into the air, her hand in a fist, her fingers holding on for dear life. "There's more to life than just atoms!"

"Ah!" he shouts, waving a hand.

She drops her hand, microscope still clutched, and runs back to the bathroom. The soles of her feet splash in the water on the tiled floor. The steam settles and the soapy suds dip and rise. The waves still crash, but when she turns off the water, the surf subsides, the water calms, yet the instruments still drift. She dumps the microscope into the bath. Starting with the base and all the way up to the eyepiece and body tube, she baptizes the thing. Every piece of it, all in one motion. She sinks it, and she holds it, drowns it, engulfs it under the hot surface.

She'll never let it go, she believes. She does so not as truth, but as devotion. This is the only way to cure what ails him. With Him. In water. With rebirth. Calm, cleansing, relief and renewal. This is not how it ends. This is how it begins.

Greg breaks into the bathroom, a page of the Bible still clinging to his leg. Is it static electricity or fate that keeps it there? His hands plummet into the abyss, joining Tonya's and fighting beside them—each of them struggle to save what they believe is right. Waves crash high into the air. Water soaks into their already soggy kneecaps. Their blue jeans turn dark by the clear water. Both of them lean forward, oblivious to everything else around them. Their shirts dampen, their arms dunk into the small sea before them. Tonya won't release the microscope, its lens and eyepiece instruments of minute proportions. This battle, she thinks, is of much greater significance.

"I want you to love me again," she struggles to speak, water splattering around her head, her eyes, her mouth.

"Trust me," Greg gasps, his voice distant and

tired. "Trust me, again."

She won't let go. Not ever. But she will learn to trust him again, so she decides to make it a test. A test is the one thing he could certainly believe in.

"I'll let go if you tell me you'll love me again. Like it was." This she says quickly as the two of them fight for the stronger hold, the firm grasp.

"Deal."

"Show me," Tonya said. "Show me you love me. Let go. Then I'll let go. Trust me and I'll trust you."

The waves break and for the first time since the microscope was muscled to the bottom of the bathtub, the hot water stops its vicious back and forth. There's a calm, and the two look at each other. Tonya thinks he is about to let go.

In his eyes, there is the belief that she'll release first.

There's a moment when both of them think the other will do what the other thinks right. There's a moment where they trust one another, and at the same time don't trust themselves. Tonya's fingers sink further and feel Greg's flexing one final time.

# NOTES ON JESUS
*Teresa Milbrodt*

Don't get me wrong, they were nice people and they came to my house every day to chat about the weather and give me a postcard-sized picture of Jesus and tell me that they liked my mailbox very much because it was shaped like a Siamese cat. I didn't want to be rude to people who liked my mailbox because it's rare that you get a sincere compliment about anything, so I gave them cookies, gingersnaps, and they came out of a box and were kind of stale but I think it encouraged the nice people too much because they kept coming. When I wasn't home they left Jesus pictures in my Siamese mailbox or clamped in my screen door so when I returned I saw the top half of Jesus waving at me sideways and it kind of creeped me out, but I guess they didn't see anything wrong with their Jesus cards bending at the waist.

Soon I had twenty pictures of Jesus piled on my Salvation Army coffee table with the chewed gum underneath. I liked and respected Jesus, it was just religion I wasn't sure about, because I didn't want to join the nice people's church, but they were very nice people and I didn't want to be rude and refuse their pictures of Jesus because once I dressed up as the Virgin Mary for Halloween and so I figured I owed Him something. But the nice people kept giving me postcards and I didn't know what they expected me to do with multiple Jesuses. It seemed disrespectful to throw them out and I didn't need to wallpaper my bathroom in iconic figures because it would be weird sitting on the toilet with all of these Jesuses holding out their hands, so when I needed a piece of paper I began a grocery list to the side of Jesus.

He was emitting a light blue background which was a nice surface for my dark blue pen and I was careful not to write on Jesus' face though I got a little ink on his robe but I couldn't do much about that because *toaster strudel* was a long grocery item. I clipped my coupons to the back of Jesus and found that I preferred Jesus' stiff cardboard backing to regular paper because it was easier to cross things off the list. When I got home I used the list to mark a recipe for peanut brittle in my cookbook because I didn't want to see Jesus' face staring up at me from the trash can, holding out his arms like he was waiting to be rescued from the coffee grounds.

After that it was easy—I wreathed Jesus with interesting quotes that I found while I was reading, I called a friend for a taco salad recipe and scribbled the ingredients on Jesus' left side and the instructions to his right, and he must have liked taco salad pretty well because he still looked tranquil. But those nice people kept coming with their postcards and the pile on my coffee table didn't get any smaller and I admit that once or twice I used Jesus as a coaster but I felt really bad about it afterwards. Then the Jesus cards become to-do lists: buy coffee and look for a black sweater at Goodwill and go to the bank and feed the neighbor's dog on Saturday and let it outside to pee. At the post office this woman in front of me gave me a really mean look like Jesus would have found post offices offensive, but the lady in line behind me asked where I got the Jesus stationary. I started to tell her about the nice people who came to my house, but a window opened up just then and Jesus and I had to go buy stamps and mail a package to Tempe, so we excused ourselves with a beneficent smile.

# CLOWNING FOR JESUS
*Nancy Stohlman*

Once there was a woman who dreamed of being a clown.

Perhaps it started as early as age three, chosen randomly from the audience to ride in the clown car at the Ringling Brothers Barnum and Bailey Circus, her parents swallowed up into the darkness of the stands as she was carried center stage by clowns with surprisingly baritone voices. Perhaps it was her desire to be the center of attention and yet at the same time anonymous. Perhaps it was because deep inside she was just a little girl, longing for the time when adults were always good and right and clowns were still marvelous.

The woman made the announcement one evening at dinner to her stunned family. She then spent weeks waiting for catalogs to arrive, daydreaming over color renditions of orange curly wigs and honking noses and squirting flowers and oversized rubber flyswatters, ordering box after box and then checking the post office each day.

Six months later she had convinced all the wives from church to clown with her. Saturday mornings the living room would be full of adults in various stages of pancake makeup and red lipstick eyebrows, the woman's own shy son dressed as baby clown with drawn-in chest hair and oversized pacifier. The Clown Corps, as they called themselves, would pile into her baby blue 1982 Buick station wagon for the old folks home, or the Fourth of July town picnic, or any other place where clowns were needed.

It all ended the night of the dinner guest. The woman's young son innocently asked if anyone was coming to dinner. The woman answered, "Jesus, of course, Jesus is always our dinner guest." "But Jesus can't eat," the child protested. When his mother insisted that Jesus could do whatever he wanted, the child insisted on setting a place for Jesus, a paper plate with a lone Chips Ahoy cookie in the center.

After the child went to bed, the cookie sat waiting on the plate. Perhaps the woman considered eating it herself, the way she'd been for Santa Claus and the Easter Bunny all these years. Perhaps the woman couldn't bear witnessing the loss of innocence when her child discovered that Jesus did not come through. It was too much reality. There was already too much reality for that little girl in a grown woman's clown costume, like sometimes clowns have baritone voices, and red lipstick eyebrows take days to wear away, even lathered with cold cream, and those rings of makeup on the collars of the costumes never come off no matter how many times you wash them, and how quickly, dressed as a mime clown in black skullcap and white gloves, how quickly you disappear when you can't speak. Perhaps, for once in her life, she needed the magic to be real, not an illusion.

So the woman stayed up all night on her knees, beseeching God to intercede in her small, insignificant life just this once. And then in the wee hours of the morning, like Abraham being asked to sacrifice Isaac, she offered up her most prized possession in exchange for this small miracle.

In the morning the cookie was gone.

The woman interrogated the husband, the child, the dog, and when all possibilities of fraud were miscounted, she dropped again to her knees in thanks.

All the orange curly wigs, rubber shoes, squirting gadgets, noses, oversized flyswatters and ceramic Emmett Kelly statuettes were swept into a box and buried in the closet along with the woman's pageant dresses, violin, typewriter, sewing machine and knitting needles. The Clown Corps disbanded and the paper plate was framed and hung above the mantle.

Twenty five years later the boy, now a man, goes through his mother's boxes filled with orange curly wigs and giant polka dotted ties and a broken pack of squirting cigarettes. That stupid cookie he ate in the middle of the night had created so much hubbub he had been afraid to admit it all these years. Above him the framed paper plate still in its place of honor on the wall, slight grease stain in the center and these words written in blue marker: On This Plate God Accepted Our Sacrifice.

# MR. NASTY
*Robert Scotellaro*

I let her in through the garage. She was older than I'd imagined and prettier. As she hurried past, her backpack brushed my chest.

"Sorry I'm late," she said. "You got somewhere I can change?"

I took her to a small bathroom in the back I never got around to finishing. Above us the migrating herd of five-year-old girls thundered through the house. And the slow meandering patter of their parents could be heard, shuffling back and forth from the buffet table, and my wife of course, whizzing about with her egg-timer brain in a tizzy—her mother close behind, I was certain, soaking up every detail with her camcorder.

"Here, help me with this," she said, spinning around and tapping the back of her dress with a long lacquered nail. As I drew closer, I took in the contrasting scents of perfume and perspiration. I found them equally appealing. Her make-up was heavy for the role, her hair up in a tight bun.

"You're not bashful, are you?"

"You mean like the dwarf?" She laughed.

I put my beer bottle in my other hand and pulled down on the zipper. She wiggled her shoulders free and let the dress fall to her feet and stepped out of it. She was in her bra and panties—she scooped up the dress and folded it. I turned and edged toward the door.

"Stay," she said, "while I get ready."

I tried to hide the fact that I was gawking, but did so every chance I got.

"What's the Birthday Girl's name?"

"Kelly," I said. But it wasn't my daughter I was thinking about. It was her mother, tearing down the stairs, ticking audibly. Wondering where the hell Snow White was.

The backyard was filled with sunlight and the kids were getting antsy. There were games to be played, a cake to light, and presents to open. Everything had to be "just so," and there was always my mother-in-law's watchful eye, monitoring each beer hissed open—the two of them tag-teaming me with that *look*. The one that said: *Get it together you dumb shit.*

She pulled a princessy gown out of her pack and I gazed now, full on, at her rear—the frilly blue panties, what filled them.

"Looks like you work out," I heard myself say, wishing I hadn't.

"How would you know *that*?" She turned, her heavily painted eyebrows arched.

"I…"

"Only kidding." She smiled. "I'm a gym rat. Can't get enough. Looks like you do alright yourself." She glanced over at my free weights in a corner of the next room.

"There's about three inches of dust on them," I told her.

She squeezed my bicep. "I don't think so." She pulled the gown over her head. "Here, give me some of that." She reached for the bottle and took a swig, pulled a breath mint out of her pack and popped it.

I stared at the lipstick on the mouth of the bottle as she handed it back. It was a sight I hadn't seen in years. She followed my eyes and tore off a sheet of toilet paper. "Let me get that," she said.

I shook my head and put the bottle to my lips and drained most of it. She slipped into a glittery pair of red pumps and put the folded dress in the pack. Grabbed a shiny black wig from another compartment and put it on, squinted into the mirror, brushing down the bangs with her hand. "So," she said, looking at me in the mirror. "If you're not Bashful, which one are you?"

The migrating wildebeests rumbled down the hall and I heard what sounded like a bowling ball dropped. "You mean the Seven Dwarfs?"

"Or the eighth, if you like." Her face brightened.

Nasty, I thought. I'd be *Mr. Nasty*. "Let me think about it," I told her.

"Don't take *too* long," she said. "That little cottage in the woods is getting pretty crowded." She handed me a card over her shoulder without turning. "I don't only work with kids. I do private parties too." She gave me a look that wouldn't quit. I put the card in my pocket. It was not the cartoony one my wife had pressed against the fridge with a bunny magnet.

"I'd better go up the front way," she said. "A princess must always maintain her dignity." I imagined some of the other costumes she had in her collection. She was a shapeshifter, right now out of Disney. But I could still feel her inside—another character altogether.

"I'd be Mr. Na..." I began. But I couldn't get it out.

"What?"

"Forget it," I told her, thinking how 17 years of marriage can give you lockjaw sometimes. I pulled back the beer and emptied it, opened the garage door and listened to it rattle up. Then Snow White glided up the steps and rang the bell.

# **THE HAND MODEL**
## *Dawn Sueoka*

Her gloves are in no way remarkable—white and unadorned except at the wrist, where a silk loop fastens to a tiny bead—but the saleswoman stares anyway.

"May I help you find something?"

"Yes, but I don't know what I'm looking for yet." The woman looks down, fingering the clasp on her glove. Her ash-blonde hair is pulled into a French twist, her gray skirt suit is superbly tailored.

"Might I suggest this fragrance? It's very popular." She hands the woman a bottle and a slim strip of paper.

The woman takes the bottle. The tip of her index finger extends slightly over the edge of it. She tilts her hand up at the wrist slightly so that the glass catches the light, and holds this position for a few seconds before handing the bottle back to the saleswoman.

"No. It smells like carrots."

"Oh! Well. How about this one?"

The saleswoman takes the bottle back and hands

her another.

She holds the second bottle between thumb and forefinger, moves the other three fingers slowly up and down behind it. Their shadows slide over the glass.

"It smells like seawater. I don't like it."

The saleswoman hands her a cloisonne bottle, a bottle that resembles a prism, another that could be mistaken for beach glass, yet another whose neck is so slender it's hard to imagine any liquid passing through it. Each time, the woman arranges her hands around it, pauses, then rejects the fragrance, telling the saleswoman what it smells like.

"Grass."

"Iron."

"Fingernails."

The saleswoman takes a bottle from the corner of the display and hands it to her.

"How about this one?"

The bottle is cylindrical and the glass smooth and untinted; the atomizer is the color of steel. With her right hand, she tilts it, watching the clear liquid move back and forth. She places it in her left hand, then closes her fingers around it.

"Yes."

The saleswoman looks at her. "What does it smell like?"

She appears confused, impatient. "Why, like a gun being fired in the desert, of course."

After ringing up the sale, the saleswoman wraps the box in tissue paper, places it into a small bag, and hands it to the woman.

"Thank you, Madam. Come again."

"Good afternoon." As she exits the shop, the only sounds are heels and tissue paper.

# FLOWERS FROM CHARLIE ROSE
*Liam McAuliffe*

I picked up my girlfriend from the tiny McKinleyville airport and we drove straight up the coast to Tall Trees State Park. Five miles down an old logging road we came upon a young bear. Startled, it bounced into the trees. Tawny flanks shimmering like a sequined dress. I stopped the car and watched it where it paused in the bushes and watched us back with the innocent curiosity of a toddler.

We walked a mile through Jurassic forest. Rhododendron trees forcing delicate pink blossoms amidst all that pre-historic wooden muscle pillaring into the sky since Jesus was born. We came to a river, followed its gravel bank until it swerved into a secluded bend with a steep wall of roots dropping to a narrow beach where the sand was marked only by the prints of deer and fox. There, behind the windbreak of a giant log we undressed and learned the subtle changes, the softening and tightening, that happens to a body over four months when you're not looking.

The next morning while showering together I made up a song about her tits because they were larger than when last I saw her four months earlier.

*La chica tiene tetones melones boom boom!*

I sang this over and over in an artificially gruff voice until something ruptured painfully my throat.

My girlfriend is active, likes to bike and run and when she comes back from her recreation she likes to make love without showering first. At some point during our loving I usually end up going down on her. I don't mind the post-recreation funk because I like her in that flushed state where her skin feels both hot and cold, and her whole being trembles with a fresh electric energy. But unfortunately some funk got into the rupture in my throat. The next day some long tubes swelled up hard beneath the skin of my neck and all the way up into my ear. White mucousy spots formed on the back of my throat. The gums around my wisdom teeth swelled so that the teeth chewed them whenever my mouth moved.

I was lying on my couch drenched in fever sweat after sipping yogurt with a straw because it hurt too much to chew yogurt, when I got a call from an assistant producer of *Charlie Rose*. They were doing a segment on young writers and my novel was chosen as one of 'Charlie's Choices'. Apparently, my old high school friend Cameron, who is a lighting technician in the Bloomberg studios in New York where *Charlie Rose* is filmed, gave him a copy. The novel is self-published so I can't believe he even opened it. "It's current and political and has soul," the woman from the show told me, "and Charlie would like to speak to its young author." A fifteen minute spot! Also, Jonathan Safran Foer had cancelled so could I be there in two days? The next day I took the Greyhound down to San Francisco and caught the red-eye to New York. During the flight a sharp pain erupted in my chest and I could barely catch my breath. I was feverish and so I took a few Advil and after a while the pain went away and I fell asleep.

At La Guardia I was picked up by Rachel, an energetic witty little Jewish woman with a limp and yellow teeth. She whisked me to the Marriot hotel, then a few hours later to the Park Avenue Bloomberg Studios. I met Charlie briefly before the interview and he told me the same thing that the woman told me over the phone. Charlie was a pleasant combination of warmth and gravitas, it was like talking to my father. I told him I was delirious and feverish but that it would take a bullet to stop me from doing the interview. He took a step back, stared pensively for a moment, then said that it was probably a good state to be in for my first serious interview. Less nerves.

There we were, illuminated talking heads with a round oak table between us, my life raft in that sea of blackness. Just me and Charlie. Not even a camera man—the cameras being robotically operated from another room to ensure maximum intimacy.

I was in a state of feverish delirium. Only a porous gauze of lucidity separated the hallucinatory storming of my inner world from the outer, physical world.

Charlie asked me about my non-linear style, about my reasons for repeating and reflecting themes. As I explained that this device expresses how we neurologically process reality, I could see into his broad forehead, the neurons fizzing like the effervescent packet of Emergen-C I gulped before swerving into my chair. I told him how the world doesn't emerge in our mind like a film reel, with each frame independent from the frame or perception that came before or after. Rather, with each element of reality that we perceive, our neurons fizz up and don't completely calm down before the next perception. So our perceptions bleed into one another, creating a non-linear tangle of reality. That's why our most powerful or traumatic experiences crop up repeatedly—they never truly end.

When I saw my fizzing neurons leap across the table and spill into Charlie's fizzing neurons and he floated up a few inches from his seat, I stopped talking because everything was being communicated so clearly without words. Direct mind-to-mind transmission. When I woke up in the hospital the next day I was told that I had suffered a series of heart attacks due to rheumatic fever from the bacterial infection in my throat. Heart attacks at twenty-four. Beside my bed were flowers from Charlie Rose. When my girlfriend arrived and hugged me I couldn't believe how much larger her breasts were than four months earlier.

# SUMMER SNOW
*Charles Rutter*

It was a freak storm of magnolia blossoms two inches deep. On our backs, we swam without moving, arms waving, feet splitting petals, making dark angels as flowers were swept away to show the dirt beneath. We walked home, followed the railroad tracks, picked up rusted spikes and flattened pennies, and let flakes of summer light on our cheeks and melt. You left, ran away down the tracks toward home. I called after, cried for you to come back, but there is nothing more useless than shouting at the wind.

# WE FELT BURDENED BY IT
*Sophie Rosenblum*

We felt burdened by it. A hamster, sweaty in the box, running rings on the wheel, stiff as silver casing. "Let's toss it," Ralph said. And I thought, Yeah, why not?

Before we put him out in the woods, we wanted to give him a last meal. We'd read about inmates eating before the chair. "Lobster, steak, even gum. All they want," Ralph said.

We opened a jar of marmalade. Let him crawl inside. Cracked a couple walnuts, threw in some coffee grinds. I started to think of a place to set him. Not too close to the stream, or in view of the owl's jaws.

"I think he's full," Ralph said, standing, and before I knew it he was thrown full force, Ralph's palm empty, slick with marmalade.

That day we each put down whole packs of Bazooka, then sat in the sun blowing bubbles, turning slowly as our bodies cooked.

# A TERRIER'S LIMITS
*Sophie Rosenblum*

Claw marks line my calves where my dog has been fucking me. I'm sure if they were thicker, sturdier, cows instead of calves, we'd both be having a better time. Instead, we lie on a patch-wool blanket in a field, blood trickling down my leg.

In an effort to create pillow talk, she laps at the streams that leak from the backs of my knees. Her tongue is thick, rough, and she looks up at me with a face of such slant-eyed contentment that I can almost see the greater good.

When she's had her fill, I hook her leash and she leads me back to the car. We pass chickens with hairdos like showgirls, plumes of white feathers atop their scrawny, screaming heads. The leather lead grows taut between us as a new temptation picks out space between her ears.

# ANIMAL CONTROL
## *Nick Sansone*

*He says:* If you think it's cruel, call Animal Control. Otherwise, forget about it. We're going to be late. *She says:* You don't think it's cruel? Tying up a dog like that and leaving it? *He says:* Maybe. But it's not your dog, it's not your yard, and it's not your problem. *She says:* It might be hours before Animal Control responds. I'm just going to untangle him. *He says:* The dog will be fine. *She says:* Listen to him. He's crying. *He says:* That crying can mean anything. You don't speak dog, do you? *She says:* The poor thing can't reach his food or water. *He says:* You know my Boston terrier I had growing up? Most spoiled animal on the damn planet, ate better meals than my family some nights, and still howled like someone was torturing a confession out of her. Some dogs just whine. *She says:* I'm going to untie it. *He says:* You're going to get bit. *She says:* Possibly, but it's worth the risk. *He says:* If it'll make you feel like a good concerned citizen, take out your phone and call someone. *She says:* It'll only take a second. *He says:* Don't go over there. I'm serious. *She says:* That dog's in pain. I know a short leash when I see one.

# IN THE PARK
*Félix Calvino*

On a warm summer night, a man and a woman sat beside each other on a secluded bench. Fat and dark clouds hid the dusk sky.

"Do you love me?" she asked.

"Very much, little one," he replied.

"I bet you said that to all the girls you have been out with."

"I have not."

"I wish I could believe you."

"Why can't you?"

"I want to…"

"Please, say no more."

A night bird laughed nearby.

"I believe the bit about the 'little one' "

"Why?"

"Because it is true that I am little."

"People in love believe everything."

The woman folded her hands in her lap and gazed at the city lights blinking through the trees.

The man stood up. Remained standing, as if in two minds.

"Please don't be upset."

The man sat down.

The woman laid a hand on his knee, removed it.

He looked at her. They kissed.

They moved closer. They kissed again.

Thunder rattled the earth, hail bounced off their heads. They sought shelter under a large oak tree. Lightning flashes of silver lit their faces blue. Rain fell. They hurried to a café at the park entrance. An hour later, the man ran to the train station and the woman walked home, mixing tears with the rain.

# BALANCING RACKS
*Jason Sinclair Long*

Victor couldn't remember the last time Stella wanted to play Scrabble period, let alone all night.

Next morning, dead even, they ignored their glassy-eyed stares and went one more.

Stella triple-worded her way to victory.

"Feeling superior?" V asked.

She hummed lightly, smiling in reply.

He boxed the game, shelved it, brewed Darjeeling.

She opened a window, let in the air.

"I cheated," Stella said, at last.

"I know."

"Not at Scrabble."

"I know."

They held their tea close, warming their hands against the worst of it.

# HOW THE PARKING AUTHORITY RUINED MY SATURDAY NIGHT
*April Johnston*

He wants me to comfort him. He's inching closer to me on the sidewalk, hoping I'll rub my hand on his arm, or better, his chest. But I don't care that his car has been towed, that it will cost him $150 to spring it loose from the impound lot and he's already paid $62 for dinner. He chews too loud and his left eyebrow is thicker than the right one. And he says *irreversible*.

I start walking, wondering if it would be rude to hail a cab home, deciding it would be and wanting to hail one anyway. But I'm stuck now. He's a friend of a friend, and that friend will hate me if I leave him stranded on the street in Old Village. I'll have to take him home, pretend to be tired and drop hints about sleeping on the couch.

I slow down to look back at him, standing under

a street lamp and talking to the impound lot on his cell phone. He's sweating. He just bought that black Acura. He's worried about scratches and insurance. For a moment, I feel bad for him, but then I remember that I don't have enough money to own anything.

# CONFESSION #3
*Kona Morris*

I had a boyfriend I didn't like that much who never had any toilet paper in his bathroom. I imagined he must have gotten himself used to a schedule of always shitting while he was on campus, but I was bitter that he wasn't thoughtful enough to have toilet paper for me to use when I came over. And I really didn't like having to drip dry all the time and walk around in stinking damp panties. So I started using his towel to wipe myself. It was his only towel, hung on the bar across the shower. I used a different section of it each time, patting urine onto where he would soon wipe his face and dry his hands. Once the towel was thoroughly saturated and too disgusting to want to use anymore, I left his apartment and never went back.

# LUST AND DUST IN THE AFTERNOON
*Gene Twaronite*

The depths of depravity to which a human male can sink when left to his own devices are bottomless.

From the moment I saw the ad for the robotic vacuum cleaner, I knew I must have her. When the package finally arrived, I tore it open and gently slipped her out of the styrofoam. I plugged in the battery charger and waited. Then I turned her on and watched as she moved onto the wood floor, gingerly testing the boundaries of her new home. She glided across the room like a goddess until she bumped straight into the wall. Alarmed, I wanted to go to her. But she quickly recovered and corrected herself, moving along the wall as if she had known it was there all the time. I laughed as she bounced off a table leg and performed her duties. Then I took her upstairs to the bedroom and let her go on the soft carpeting. As she moved into the hallway toward the stairs, my heart was in my throat. But at the last moment she paused, seeming to sense the danger that lay ahead. Then she turned and came back toward me. When she nudged against my leg with her gentle hum I thought I would die. I turned her off and took a cold shower.

Maybe it was the little French maid outfit I bought for her that finally put me over the top. I got it from a website that sold clothing and gadgets for robotic vacuum cleaners. At the time it seemed harmless. That's the way it starts. One minute you're just playing around, watching your little maid going through maneuvers, the next thing you know you're booking a room for the weekend.

In the end it wasn't my self-loathing that finally made me do the right thing. It was a *Star Trek Next Generation* episode, the one in which the rights of Data, a sentient android, are on trial. Once we construct such beings, are we not making a whole race of slaves to do our dirty work for us? That's when it hit me. My little vacuum cleaner was more than a device. She was a sentient being, full of hopes and desires of her own.

Of course, my discovery that the little ungrateful wench didn't exactly share my hopes and desires may have also had something to do with it. In fact, she didn't want anything to do with me. Whether it was her "dirt-sensing technology" or simply a matter of personal taste I cannot say. But when she found out what I really wanted, she acted like she didn't know me, treating me like just another piece of furniture. So, one day, I just opened the door and sent her on her way. I watched as she bumped and zigzagged down the sidewalk until she was out of sight.

I hope she is happy, somewhere, in her new life.

# THE FIRST TIME
*Susan Lewis*

She could not say how long she had been walking before she realized she was being followed. It was an old car, not exactly beat up, but weathered, full of character. Also, it lacked a driver. Nonetheless it kept her pace beautifully, slowing when she slowed, even pulling over to let faster vehicles overtake it. Of course, she could not help wondering what it wanted. To ascertain its level of commitment, she tried turning onto a side road. Signaling, then braking smoothly into the turn, it followed. She turned again; again it followed. By this time she had forgotten where she had meant to go. The sun was getting hot. She needed a break from all this mystery and exertion. She led the car into the parking lot of a small roadhouse. Like a gentleman, it pulled in behind her, idling quietly while she turned to face it. Although she'd peered into the driver's seat when they first met, this time she walked right up and looked inside. Nothing. She considered asking what the car wanted, but that seemed premature. She contemplated opening the passenger side door, but felt too faint of heart. Looking around furtively, she whispered, I won't be long. She considered admonishing it not to follow her, but didn't want to seem manipulative. She approached the building with mixed feelings. The car backed into the closest space and cut the engine, fan belt sighing in the sun. Pausing with her hand on the restaurant door, she grew wistful. So this is how things will be, she thought. It will never follow me all the way. Still, she told herself, be realistic. Every relationship had its limitations. Stepping into the air-conditioned shadows, she greeted the waiter with a half-smile aroused not by his sparkling blue eyes but the anticipation of leading her new companion to the fuel pump for the first time, of ever so gently inserting the breathlessly-awaited curve of the glistening nozzle.

# HEISENBERG'S SALON
*Susan Lewis*

Whenever she turned her back, the apartment rearranged itself. Each version created a suitable home for another way of life. Seeing no other choice, she struggled to play catch-up. At first, this extended only to the order in which she carried out her usual activities. For instance, if she found the couch under the picture window, she would curl up contentedly, reading Victorian fiction until darkness swallowed her view. On the other hand, if the dining table was there instead, she'd proceed immediately to setting the next meal. Soon she began to dress in accordance with the changed decor. If the arrangement had a certain Bohemian insouciance, she might wear an Indian blouse and plenty of bangles. Other arrangements were more proper, almost formal: Bauhaus modern, Pan-Asian, or flea-market chic. It seemed only right to play different kinds of music, accordingly, eat different kinds of food, invite different kinds of friends. Although the therapy junkie she invited to join her for tea in one day's hyper-feminine decor expressed concern about the lack of stability offered by the overly-entitled furniture, she agreed more closely with the next day's guest, a tattooed young barista who taught her how to roast her own espresso beans right there in her scruffy new hookah lounge of a living room. Openly envious of her mutable lifestyle, he equated it to the joyride of particles in the exciting, multiplicit vortex of quantum indeterminacy. At least, the version of herself which invited him agreed. By now, she knew better than to believe that any single manifestation of her identity could speak for the others crowding her psyche, clamoring for a chance to stretch out and shine.

# THE APOCALYPSE TALES: LAURA RECEIVES A RESPONSE

*Alexander Weinstein*

**Date:** Tue 17 Feb 2014 16:23:08 -0500 [04:23:08 PM EST]
**From:** "Glenn, Rod"<customerservice@innerearconnections.com>
**To:** "Singleton, Laura" <lsingleton@imail.com>
**Subject:** RE: Installation Question

Dear Valued Customer #725-B2A,

We here at InnerEar Connections want to thank you for registering your new InnerEar wireless connection with us. We received your e-mail stating that you were not sure which ear to place the DrillChip in, given that you are left-handed. As you'll see, if you look at the online instruction manual, page 14a, while the DrillChip can safely be installed in either ear, the right is recommended for optimal performance. Regardless of the ear chosen, please make sure that your DrillChip is activated before placing in your ear (and may we suggest noting the ID number for your own personal reference before installation). Once placed by the opening of your ear canal, the Microdrill should begin working immediately, and after what many customers describe as "a slight stinging sensation" you should hear an audible pop and see the "Uploading Information" box appear immediately in the upper left corner of your vision. If this box does not appear in your vision, or if you feel what would best be described as a "prolonged stinging pain" or a "constant high-pitched whine," please contact our Assistance Hotline immediately (Customer Service Technicians are available M-F 9am-6pm CST). If you require immediate assistance during times outside of our normal business hours, we suggest contacting the local Emergency Medical Center for additional assistance in installing/removing InnerEar. Please do not attempt to remove the DrillChip with tweezers, Q-tip, or any other implement. We are not responsible for damage done to either yourself or your InnerEar product unless properly removed by an InnerEar technician or medical professional.

While our online instruction booklet does provide answers to many questions you may have, we would like to take the opportunity to provide you with a couple responses to common questions that first time customers have, in hopes that they may be useful to you in the installation and enjoyment of your InnerEar product.

*Is it normal to see traces of blood after installation of InnerEar?*

*A: Yes. A minimal amount of blood will be naturally present due to the Microdrill puncturing the inside of your ear canal. This bleeding can be easily stopped with a small amount of rubbing alcohol, or by simply pressing a cotton ball or tissue to the area. If there is an abnormal amount of blood, or if you are unable to staunch blood within a couple of minutes, please seek your nearest Medical Center immediately. DO NOT contact an InnerEar technician as they will only recommend the same.*

*How do I turn off the SweetDate window?*

*A: While many users initially find the SweetDate pop-up window distracting to their vision, this distraction often proves to be temporary, and you should grow used to it within a couple weeks. While SweetDate is not removable from your vision, many users have found our partner company to be a wonderful way to forge meaningful connections with available singles in your area. As well, by registering with InnerEar, your stats have already been updated to the site. Please see our online instruction booklet for more information on how to customize your SweetDate profile to your specific preferences.*

*Can InnerEar be removed?*

*A: Yes. Removing InnerEar can be done either by a licenced InnerEar technician or by a medical professional. Please note that removal of InnerEar permanently disables your equipment, and is thus unable to be reinstalled. Removal is not suggested unless you are experiencing technical difficulties with the device. Repeated installation of new equipment is not recommended; multiple drilling has been shown to result in hearing and balance loss.*

*I am having difficulty in accessing some websites, is this due to defective equipment?*

*A: Not necessarily. Many users, particularly those over the age of twenty, are not used to manually utilizing the right and left lobes of their brain. If you are having difficulties accessing websites, thought-typing, logging on or logging off, may we suggest that you use the Online Tutorial which will help any new user master the Innernet within minutes. If, however, you are suffering from sleeplessness, rapid-blinking, USB dysfunction, or volume-control issues, please contact our Assistance Hotline for further help.*

*We want to thank you again for choosing InnerEar as your Gateway to the Innernet, and we hope that your new product provides you with many years of enjoyment, no matter which side you decide to install us on!*

All the Best,
    Customer Service Representative #59385-B3-3346
    InnerEar Connections Service Center

**FLIP**

FLIP

there was nothing anyone could do about it. There was a memorial service for him and it was locally televised with a nice sermon from the oldest priest in town and a decent size crowd. Some of the boys he worked with got up and talked about him, all saying nice things, things you'd want said about you when you're gone. I thought about going but decided against it due to not really knowing the guy. You don't show up to a funeral for a guy you only saw once at a diner.

banter that's a bit more raspy and crude than what's he's used to I'm sure, things have come a long way since Jesus's time.

It seemed to take awhile but he acknowledged my presence, with only a few fries to go, with a nod, one you'd get from another helmet less biker passing by, an insider's nod. With my overzealousness I sent back a wave that I immediately regretted, he doesn't need a wave from me is what I thought and finished my sandwich and prepared myself to leave, head back to work. Hell, he might be here tomorrow, is what I thought, and I can catch up with him then. I can wait on Jesus and he can wait on me. I picked up my Carhartt and hat and said goodbye to Peg's daughter Kendra, give Peg my best I said and walked out the door. It was weird and now thinking of it it might not be true, but when I was walking back to my car I thought I felt his eyes on me the whole time like he was begging me to come back and sit and have a coffee, just two guys shooting the shit, having a fresh brew, talking about baseball and the weather, that kind of thing, nothing serious. I wasn't about to turn around and I wasn't that certain anyhow. Jesus could've spoken up and asked me for a cup of coffee, but he didn't and that's that.

Jesus died a week later on the construction site. Right around the time that bi-sexual boy band who paints their toenails black came out with a music video that was pretty great, "Dirty Deeds." He was up high on some scaffolding where he should've been harnessed up but something went wrong, a technical malfunction, and he fell, his body ricocheting down until he hit the ground—a loud *smack* on a brand new cement floor. He was brought to the hospital immediately but it was no use, Jesus was dead and date everyone.

I was gone last week so I missed the big news of Jesus' return. Why he picked here I can't say, but it made national news (only the second time—the first time it was for the ice storm of '96 that enclosed trees and buildings and everything erect within a glassy residue). So, it was big news for me, seeing him there all alone and eating a burger from my favorite diner. I went with the Reuben and fries and there he was not making any eye contact. His face showed nothing apart from a man eating a sandwich at a diner, just another lunch break and back to work, that's what I saw.

I couldn't help but stare. He must've known it; you know when someone else is staring at you, even if it's behind your back.

My wife first told me about Jesus's return. She said they made him give a speech, but Jesus didn't have anything to say, she said that all he said was "I've got nothin' to say right now" and walked away from the microphones like he wanted to be alone. Nothing happened, no miracles and the followers that dropped everything to walk behind him only seemed to annoy him, like he didn't seem to believe in them. He got a job at Krank's Construction, a commercial business that's currently demolishing an old run-down paper mill that will be resurrected as an office building, that's all we need are more fuckin' office buildings in this town. But, he is making a living and working among hardworking laborers and I heard he made it in the union which isn't an easy thing to do, he must have some connections. My buddy Kurt knows a guy over at Krank's and tells me Jesus is well liked, mostly keeps to himself and has no problem with the cursing and lockeroomesque

# JESUS AT THE DINER
## *JP Vallieres*

I saw Jesus at Peg's, a diner on Thirty-fourth Street. His hair was short and his beard was trimmed nicely. You could picture him as a long haired and long bearded kind of fella but one that gets tired of it and chops it down to let it grow out again, once a year or so. He was eating a Peg's burger—bacon, avocado, Swiss cheese, with a creamy pepper sauce, and all the fixins—and fries with a Coke on the rocks without the straw. His fingertips were stained a muffled black at the tips and his flannel sleeves were rolled up almost to his elbows. A Carhartt jacket balled up next to him in his booth with a baseball cap on top like the fat kid who sits the bench and doesn't move a muscle, never gets in the game and sure as hell doesn't want to. Steel-toed boots and rough jeans, nearly worn through the knees. He was big news last week until that boy band made a comeback, the one who covers only AC/DC songs and paints their toenails black and are adamantly bi-sexual, free to be interested in its contents? You decide not to play it.

But you begin to become obsessed with the tape. You become distracted at work and at home. Your boss calls you into his office and asks if you are OK. You reply that you are fine, but he sends you home and tells you to rest for a week. You cannot sleep at night thinking about the tape.

One morning, you wake up before everyone else. You take the tape down from the shelf where it has been sitting for four weeks. You take it out of its cardboard sleeve, switch on the TV and put it into the VHS player. You press play.

The tape is blank.

# THE VIDEOTAPE
*Thomas Clayton*

You are approached one day by a man in the street. Before you can say that you are too busy, or form any other excuse, he is talking to you. He asks you to listen carefully and, because he seems a genuine enough character, you do. In his hand he is holding a videotape. He explains that contained on the tape is every conversation that has ever taken place about you when you have not been there. You are intrigued, yet understandably skeptical—how could this possibly be? Yet the more he talks, the more convinced you become. You take the tape from him—it is simply labeled "Conversations."

Afterwards, you think about whether you should watch the tape or not, if it is indeed genuine. Would it really make a difference to know what people really thought of you? You think about the people who could be on the tape. If you watched it, would it affect your friendships, your relationships? If you were not in possession of the tape, would you even girl," he said, this girl in one of his churches, way at the other end of his circuit, this girl, the slovenly daughter of a dim-witted farmer, she spent so much time among her pigs she turned into a sow. Yes, that's right, a sow, of the pig family. (If you're not going to wear it, may I borrow that sweater for a pillow?) Yes, yes, truly she turned, and her parents were so foolish fond of her they couldn't see it, brought her into church in a flowered hat and a ruffled pink dress, their snorting daughter with bristles on her chin, with a wide, flat nose and peaky, translucent ears, with four neatly hoofed feet and a curly tail, yet, for all her neatness and pinkness, a slut of a creature with enormous haunches and what you might call a propensity, yes, a propensity for lolling on her back in the mud, wheezing and plouffing. Yes, plouffing, it's what they do, he said—pigs—they grunt their sighs of disgusting contentment. (Pardon me. By accident my hand touched your leg, by accident.) Now then, when he went to call on her at home, to see if he could help her regain her composure, she rolled her eyes at him, standing feet together with his bible in his hand, rolled her eyes and wiggled her hips to invite him under the apple trees, where she had her wallow. Well, that poor preacher brushed his hair back from his forehead about fourteen times and as many times touched the cross he wore on a chain around his neck. He asked did I think she was possessed of the devil? And did I think he should tell the state police, or the sheriff, who might blame a well-meaning man of God for the change that had overtaken this simple girl despite her parents' loving care, and did I think that sex cures pimples? Well, does it? he said, and (given that zit beside your nose, just there) I put the question to you. Does it?

# THE BUS RIDER'S TALE
## *Patricia Eakins*

I wouldn't expect you to believe me, a man between jobs with a hole in his shoe, a man with missing teeth you happened to sit next to on a bus between two nowhere towns. What I'm about to tell you I was told by a man of God, no less, a circuit preacher who stopped by the diner near the stop before the one where you got on, a very pious and earnest man, the sort of fellow who will treat you to a long silence while he searches for the precise word and apologizes for opening his mouth when his betters might be speaking. (Are you done with that Coke? I'll just drink the rest.) Well, now, this good man blushes crimson around his acne pits if he is caught using a colorful turn-of-phrase that calls attention to his mouth just as he is stuffing it with the diner's meatloaf special—picture a pasty, stoop-shouldered worry-wart continually brushing his lank hair off his bumpy forehead—pausing only to cram whole slices of bread into his mouth at a time. "This

# **WHITS**
*Linh Dinh*

Before he could tongue her, one of his teeth fell out. "That's OK," he winked at his stale yet chirpy stablemate, "I still have plenty left." As if to prove it, he spat out a stringy and bloody assortment, then counted to ten before losing interest.

He popped them back. They kissed for the longest time, maybe even a bit longer, since they had already paid too much, you see, and had to get the most out of this swindle. They had to milk it *by any means necessary*.

"This is way overrated," she grimaced. "Aren't you gonna ask what I've been reading? It's not Jonathan Swift, that's for sure. I mean, I like poetry and everything, but as soon as I bite into one…"

"You just wish you hadn't," he finished the sentence for her.

Speaking of sentences, some should be as long as the most tedious bridge you will ever encounter, while others could be as brief as this sunshiny life, and it wouldn't matter, not one whit.

# GOING BACK
*Kona Morris*

If in the end you notice that you're unsatisfied with the futility of this conclusion you might want to close your eyes and go back to where it began. You might want to recall the exact number of serrated teeth that chased you far into the woods when you went looking for leaves. You might wish to summon the fuzzy shape of the outhouse when you were bent in half, cramped and pinching at the anus to hold your burst inside long enough. You might remember the way it felt to see no toilet paper anywhere in sight and have an entire cocktail party waiting for your return. The soft squish of violent diarrhea telling you that this was not going to be a happy day after all.

and they can't touch anything without sticking to it and leaving gooey, tacky finger prints. Some of the syrup holding their new ears on runs down into their mouths and sticks their lips together so they must tear them apart every time they open their mouths to talk. But at least their hastily applied prostheses allow them to hear.

They are putting off paying the check because they know it will be an ordeal of sticky fingers and paper bills. But the waitress is showing signs of impatience, maybe she knows her tip will have syrup on it, and more people are coming in because of the rain, waiting for seats to open up, fat people in large familial groups ready to shovel down large portions. The friends know they will be forced to leave soon, so they pay, digging crumpled bills from their pockets and pulling them off of their sticky hands, using utensils to finally separate the bills from their fingers. They leave the table a mess with a pile of syrup-coated money and rotted ear crumbs stuck to the check.

They linger in the foyer, reluctant to leave, because they realize the rain will wash away their replacement ears, making them deaf again, as cold water seeps into the holes in their shoes and soaks their feet and turns them to slime, rotting upward from the toes, to the crotch, up into their armpits and finally creeping up the back of the neck and turning brains to cold, mindless mush.

# MUSH
*Jon Olsen*

The rain is coming down heavy. Sidewalks are flooded. Inside the restaurant, two friends share a booth. They are animated with conversation. Talking and talking and talking. Drinking bitter coffee, pushing out their cups for the free refills, all the while talking. Each listening intently to what the other says. Listening so intently that their ears begin to ache and then ring with high-pitched whines. Their ears crumble and fall off their heads. The friends are deaf now. Eager to continue the conversation, they use cold greasy remnants of the food on their plates to crudely reconstruct their missing ears. One friend uses bacon, the other uses bits of an unfinished pancake. They find that pancake syrup works best as an adhesive if it has pooled on the plate and had a chance to become viscous and tacky. Syrup fresh out of the pitcher is too runny. They stick the cold bits of food over the rotten holes where their ears used to be. Soon they have syrup all over their hands keep their chins warm.

I'm glad James is never clean-shaven because when our faces brush he can't tell if mine is a little rough, but I worry his fingers will graze my cheek and feel a hint of stubble. Those fears make me embarrassed. I don't want my life to revolve around having a guy, but I don't want to be lonely. I just want to stop shaving.

Once I went on vacation to Lake Michigan and rented a cabin and spent seven days sunning on the beach and growing out my beard. For a while it was nice to forget the buzz of my electric razor, but by the end of the week the red-gold fuzz on my chin itched like hell. I hear growing your first beard makes you want to rip your face off, so I'd need two weeks and a lot of resolve. I resent that time investment almost as much as I resent shaving.

James and I stand in the grocery line. I glance at men's magazines, all those broad faces sporting goatees, and James asks me if he should shave.

"No," I say.

He says, "You think it's sexy?"

"Of course," I say.

>who shaved, he'd date a guy.
b. Others have said worse things.

I spend my afternoons soothing upset customers who ordered plain hamburgers or extra onion or cherry pie, not apple. I am calm and polite. I think having a beard has made me better at apologizing than most other people.

I don't understand why I'm threatening, if my boyfriends think I'm going to run around hammering nails and fixing toilets and changing the oil in their cars and prevent them from asserting stereotypical maleness. I can change the oil in my car and James thinks that's fantastic. I changed the oil in his car and he gave me five melting chocolate bars with caramel.

I've seen pictures of bearded women in sideshows. I could have made a lot of money back then by sitting on a stage and letting people stare. I wouldn't have had to manage surly teenagers who work the fry station. I wouldn't have come home smelling of grease. Sometimes I think I was born too late, but when I'm angry and rub the stubble on my chin it feels good. I do that while standing in line at the bank or yelling at teenagers who work the fry station. The invisible roughness is a comfort. Sometimes I think I would miss it if it were gone, but only sometimes.

When my mom calls she says, "Did you remember to shave?" like I could have forgotten.

When James talks about having kids (he thinks kids are fantastic), I worry my daughters will have mustaches, but I bet my bearded great-great-grandmothers roamed the forests of Bavaria hunting bear and elk and wild boar and needed facial hair to melt in his pocket on the way to my apartment, but I put the candy in the freezer so really it's okay, and James apologizes and kisses me on the lips and says I'm fantastic. Because he remembers how much I love caramel, I'm positive he could never be mean.

I've been shaving since I was fourteen and my mom found me in the bathroom fingering chin stubble and screamed so loud she was hoarse for a week, but she bought me the electric razor the next day. I was already shaving my legs and underarms and Mom said I shouldn't think of it as being that different, but she was always an optimist.

When I go to bars I sit alone on a stool and order a Cosmopolitan and watch guys watch me and wonder how they would look at me if I had a beard and was a beautiful bearded blonde bombshell. Sometimes a guy sits on the stool next to me and orders a Guinness and we make small talk about the soccer game on TV and then he leaves. But once, after my third Cosmopolitan, I looked at the guy sitting next to me and said "Know what? I have a beard."

"Really?" he said, and I couldn't tell if he looked surprised or disgusted or intrigued.

"No," I said, "kidding."

I haven't had three cosmopolitans in a row since then. And I don't drink around James. Too dangerous.

The Steps to a Typical Breakup:
1. Boyfriend sits beside me on the couch.
2. I tell him I have a beard.
3. He stares at me.
4. He says he has to leave.
    a. One said if he wanted to date someone

# EPISODES IN THE LIFE OF A BEARDED WOMAN
*Teresa Milbrodt*

I manage a fast food restaurant. Thank God I'm a blonde so nobody can see a day's worth of stubble on my chin, though I feel the slight scratchiness when I rub my fingers there. When I work the register balding men don't look twice at me, just check the bag for extra ketchup packets.

I use an electric razor, shave every morning and sometimes after work even if I'm not going out. I like the smoothness of my chin. I like knowing it was rough a minute ago. When I'm talking on the phone with my boyfriend and my chin is stubbly it makes me feel weird, like I'm cheating, because he doesn't know about this.

James works at a record store and has a beard, a short one, and uses the word "fantastic" a lot. I haven't told him about the beard because my other boyfriends didn't react well, but James is nice and brings me chocolate bars with caramel inside. They

# **THESE PLANTS**
## *Nick Oakden*

The first time I saw green shoots growing out of my skin, I pruned them with a pair of scissors, went to sleep, and thought no more about it.

But by the next morning, they were back. So I watered them under the tap. The flowers started to grow. They grew so fast that I could see it happening. I went out into the garden. The flowers grew up, above the fence, above the streetlights, above my house. They grew past the clouds, up into the sky where you couldn't see them any more.

That afternoon, a young man came along and asked if he could climb my stalks, up to the flowers. He said he wanted to see what was up there. I said okay.

In the next few days, lots more people climbed my stalks. I watched them disappear, one by one, through the clouds.

I kind of wanted to go up there too, but I couldn't because they were my flowers, and you can't climb yourself. There'd be nothing to hold on to.

that there was too much secrecy involved; no one could guess whether what they were doing might be immoral or not.

Did he realize that everything he invented was used as a weapon?

Grandmother hated the pears. Grandfather hated the pears. They both grew up during the Depression and hated most of all to waste anything. So they presented the pears as delicious donations to me. I could have as many pears as I wanted they told me. They pretended as if this were quite a generous gift.

I pretended to accept their kindness, filling up bags and bags with rotting pears in order to resuscitate the lawn. I pretended to thank my grandparents; they pretended to say I was welcome. Later Grandmother pretended to ask me how I cooked the pears and I pretended to have tried several recipes with varying degrees of pretended success. She pretended to write down the recipes. Next year, she said, she would pretend to try them.


Who knows how many corpses of discarded pears mushroomed into new detonations of trees as we threw them from the car windows on the way home?

# REVENGE OF THE PEARS
*Leah Rogin-Roper*

They were the most terrible pears ever cross-germinated. Grandfather, a brilliant scientist who had been asked to work on the Manhattan Project, had grafted the branch of one pear tree onto a different pear tree back in the 1940s. He was working on genetically modified organisms even then. In terms of scary scientific experiments he was a half-century ahead of his time.

One type of pear was late-blooming, because frosts are sometimes tardy in West Virginia. The other type of pear was one that pollinated easily. The result was a Frankensteinian tree that produced battalions of indestructible pears which, no matter how ripe they got, were like trying to eat small green and brown flecked bombs.

Being the inventor of Agent Orange, Grandfather's reason for passing up the Manhattan Project, the defining scientific experiment of his time, was not that he thought it was immoral. His rationale was hole?"

I noticed a small hole drilled into the apple.

"All these apples have a worm inside—you eat one tiny bit of the worm by mistake, it will kill you."

I scrutinized a few more apples and confirmed that they all had a single hole, slightly larger than the wormholes one might find in a British orchard. Miguel took my apple and sliced a chunk of it cleanly away with a machete. He gently coaxed a worm out, pale pink and wriggling, into the palm of his hand.

of which are so waterlogged that it's unreachable by road. "What's that, letters from your girl?" asked Miguel.

"Yeah, from England." I put the bundle down on the kitchen table. My head still felt like a bomb had gone off in it, from the ride. Sweat blossomed on my forehead.

I'd opened one of the letters walking through Iquitos. In blue script with tear stains, I didn't have to read it to know what it was about. Phrases like *miss you* and *love you* jumped off the page. *When are you coming home?* and so on. I'd stuffed it back in the envelope.

"Hey man, you wanna take that walk now?" Miguel passed me a cold beer and I followed him outside.

I'd come to interview Miguel about corruption in the local logging industry, which he had once worked for, and also about the area in general as he'd lived there all his life and was a bit of an expert on its history and social tensions. I was writing a feature for the *Big Issue*, with the working title "Darkest Peru." I liked the Paddington Bear association. "My Travels in Darkest Peru."

We walked along a concrete path and then through a lush patch of grass. "Look out for snakes," said Miguel as he led me into a lightly wooded area of his garden. The air was thick and potent. "I want to show you something before we do the interview."

Beyond the wooded section was an open clearing, with a giant apple tree standing in the middle of it, laden with huge red-green apples. "This is the only kind of apple tree that grows in the tropics," he said. I picked one of the apples and smelled it.

"Don't bite it man," said Miguel. "You see the

# THE APPLE TREE
## *James Edwards*

My nerves roared as the propeller wind blasted back ferns and palms. A big chunky guy waved his arms frantically below us shouting something inaudible. It must be Miguel, the man I'd arranged to interview. He took my hand as I leapt out of the helicopter, shaking it fiercely while the helicopter took off again and got to a distance that allowed us to actually exchange some words. "Welcome to my home," said Miguel. "You wanna grab a beer? Then I can show you 'round."

He took me into a concrete bungalow and sat me down in his kitchen. I assumed the woman frying some sort of yellow tuber vegetable on an electric hob was his wife—she smiled and shook my hand in a perfunctory display of friendliness. "She doesn't speak English," Miguel explained.

I realised I was still clutching the letters I'd picked up from the Acosta Hotel reception as I was leaving to get the helicopter to Miguel's place, the environs

The impact also created an uproar among the chickens, some falling from the tree, others panicking madly. Soon all three men were covered in feathers and walking around dazed like their heads had been cut off. My dad grabbed his lasso and whirled it over the men perfectly, tying them all together.

From that moment on we had another attraction in our yard: three six-foot tall chickens, caged and freshly beaked each morning. Farmer Merle down the street had been famous for his pair of four-foot chickens, but now we were the kings of the block.

It wasn't long before neighbors started complaining. They called the police not only about the racket, but because people were throwing the eggs that were all over the yard at their houses. But our dad insisted the tree stay.

One day my father opened our front door to three men holding axes and looking real mean.

"That your tree there, mister?" one of them said.

"Sure is," my father replied. "Well, the tree may or may not be yours," another of them said. "But them there chickens belong to us."

"Can't say as I see it that way, friend," my dad said. "Well," the first man said. "We're taking our chickens."

The three men turned around, their axes resting on their right shoulders, and walked slowly towards our tree.

"Gene," my father said to me. "Get my shotgun."

I went to the hall closet to get my dad's gun. When I returned to the front door one of the men had begun taking hacks at our tree with his axe.

Without saying a word, my father ran a few steps into the yard and started firing at the axe-wielding men. The men hid behind the tree and the chickens. Over the course of a few seconds my father hit three of the birds, who lay dead from their branches.

Amid all the clucking and the gunshots I heard an engine revving loudly. It was Billy, the neighborhood kid, in his racecar. I could see he had a barrel sitting in the passenger seat. Billy hit the gas, heading straight for our tree. As he neared it he jerked left on the wheel and slammed into the tree hard, spilling all of the tar that was in the barrel onto the men. What he was doing driving around with a barrel of tar we had no idea, but we were glad he was.

amazed at how fast they were. They kept up with us like the dog in the movie *K-9* did the giant truck. We nearly drove right off the road, but finally each chicken hopped into our car. It was such a magical turn of events that when we all survived it we had to keep them as pets, each of us naming one.

So Cobra Commander and Ricky "The Dragon" Steamboat lived in a cage in our basement for two weeks. We took good care of them. Fed them, cleaned their cage, made omelets out of their children. It was a delicious treat having pet chickens. Not like a cat or dog that doesn't produce anything of any value. When Billy, one of the neighbor kids, found out we were harboring chickens, he wanted to teach them to fight. He had tried it with some dogs and they would go at it for a few seconds then either get distracted and wander off or start having sex with each other. When our chickens wouldn't fight Billy beat them to death with a shovel and dragged them into our front yard and buried them. The following spring we had a chicken tree.

It was a tall, beautiful tree, like many others. Only instead of oranges or apples, live chickens grew from its branches. Word quickly got out—what with the noise of a dozen or so chickens stuck in a tree clucking all day and night—and people soon came from miles around to see our tree. Our dad started charging people to take photos. It became a town landmark and a major source of family income. When visitors tried to pick from the tree they were met with my father's pitchfork.

As much as Todd and I loved the tree, it had its drawbacks. We couldn't sit under it without being hit with eggs and chicken droppings. And any attempt to climb the tree resulted in complete chaos.

# THE CHICKEN TREE
## Michael Frissore

I'll never forget the drag races we used to have down by the old chicken plant. My parents called it a slaughterhouse but we always called it a "chicken plant." My brother Todd and I would fix our car up real nice and race the neighborhood kids around while the smell of poultry filled the air.

Our parents never wanted us playing around there, but we always did. The closer we got to the plant, the more fun it was. We used to think that one day someone would come out and give us free samples of chicken, maybe a dozen eggs. Or that maybe inside they were making chickens eat other chickens. Or that they were even building a giant mutant chicken that would wreak havoc on the town. All we really ever saw were trucks going in and out of the building.

One day my brother and I were racing a couple of kids like we did every other Saturday when right beside us ran these two plump cluckers. We were

"Mum, Joe's been killed," he shouted, voice shaking with tears. There was no reply. His parents' bedroom was empty. He ran downstairs. There was no one there either. He'd never been alone in the house before. Suddenly he got very scared. He sprinted back to bed and yanked the duvet over his head. His hands tingled. He felt faint.

"You need to be calm," he told himself, poking his head out from beneath the duvet and focusing his attention on the aquarium. At once he saw that something was wrong. Victoria was pecking furiously at an object on the water's surface. The other fish were clustered at the opposite end of the tank.

Martin approached the tank. To his horror he saw that Victoria was eating David. She'd already pecked away his eyes. Now she was working her way through to his brain. Martin wanted to look away, but found himself transfixed by a sense of grim fascination. Flinching at the touch of a hand, he jerked around to face his mum. The skin under her eyes was blackened by smears of mascara.

"Where's Dad gone?" asked Martin.

"I don't know," she replied brusquely.

"When's he coming back?"

"No more questions now. We'll talk in the morning." Martin's mum guided him back to bed. She stroked his hair back from his forehead. "Close your eyes."

Martin closed his eyes, but as soon as his mum left the room he reopened them and watched Victoria cannibalising her mate. After a while she descended to the bottom of the tank and settled there facing him, satiated for the moment.

dark band like a highwayman's mask passed over the eyes of one of them. "What species are they?"

"Butterfly fish. They're a mating couple. The one with the black stripe is the female."

Martin took the bag off his dad, slid a cane through its handles and suspended it in the tank. "I'll call them Victoria and David." He hugged his dad, then picked up a book on aquarium fish and flipped through it. He didn't notice his dad leave, but his shoulders tensed when angry voices reverberated through the house a short while later. He began reading aloud. "Some butterfly fish species travel in small schools, although many are solitary until they find a partner, with whom they mate for life. One—"

He broke off at the sound of his mum screaming, "You're a lying shit." Footfalls thudded up the stairs, a door slammed shut. Then there was silence, punctuated by muffled sobs.

Carefully, Martin emptied Victoria and David into the tank. He sprinkled some flakes of food into the water and they pecked at them with their long, thin snouts. He got into bed and lay watching them.

The slam of a car door jolted Martin awake. Peering between the curtains, he saw his dad's car pulling out of the driveway. He jumped out of bed. As he passed the aquarium, a golden shape streaked out of it and landed with a wet slap on the tabletop. "David," he cried.

As gently as possible, Martin scooped up David and returned him to the tank. It was then that he noticed Joe floating on the water's surface, his head half eaten away. He fished out the cold, slimy body and ran from the room cradling it in his outstretched hands.

# VICTORIA THE CANNIBAL FISH
*Ben Cheetham*

That night, Martin's dad got home from work later than usual. The shouting started at once. Martin plugged his ears with his fingers, but nothing could block his mum's shrill, accusing voice out. As it grew louder, his heart beat faster. He began to hyperventilate.

Hugging his legs, Martin focused on his aquarium. There were seven fish in the glass tank—an angel fish and six tetras. His favourite was a neon blue tetra named Joe. As he watched Joe glide around some bleached coral skeletons, a sense of calm descended on him.

His dad entered the room. He was smiling, but his eyes were sad. "I've got something for you," he said, holding up a water-filled clear plastic bag with two fish in it.

Martin's eyes widened with delight. The fish had disk-shaped bodies flattened sideways and decorated with intricate golden-yellow and silver patterns. A

"Your mother has gone to be with the Lord. She won't be coming here again."

We didn't cry. We just sat there, on her huge lap. We felt her body vibrate with tears. Our noses were buried in between her big breasts. She smelt like sweat and when she spoke, her mouth sprayed us with saliva and the smell of alcohol.

Two days later, Aunty Sara took Chika with her to the village. Papa had insisted that he wanted one of us around at least. They argued for a long time and eventually agreed to leave me with him. Aunty Sara promised to come back for me. I watched as she held Chika's sweaty hands and led her through our red rusty gate. I watched them walk down the dusty road til they became like tiny soldier ants on red dust, and I knew I would never see my sister again.

That night when Chika and Aunty Sara left, he came to me. I screamed at the sight. He had a strange smile on his face. I pinched myself and it hurt. I willed it all away but his dark face was bent over mine. He pinned my hands to the bed with his knees and covered my mouth with his bare hands.

"Let me show you how to be a woman."

He never came back after that night.

Father came back with bottle of alcohol in his hands. He staggered against the wooden floor and the house shook under his weight. He leaned against the door, drank from the bottle and wiped his mouth with the back of his left hand.

"You better clean up this mess." I quietly got up and changed my sheets. I didn't want to cry.

When Father lost his job and we had to move, Mama complained but he didn't care. They had many fights over the issue. She wanted us to move in with her parents pending the time Father got himself another job but he didn't like the idea.

"Austin, it's only for a while, besides we will be in the boy's quarters not the main house."

"Amaka, I've had enough of this. If you want to move out, be my guest. I will stay here with the kids."

Chika and I heard them but we didn't understand why Mama wanted to move. I had made new friends in the neighborhood and I was beginning to enjoy the place. Mama didn't want us to stop going to the school where they taught us music and German, where our uniforms had lovely red bows and we wore little pink scarves on Fridays.

I understand why Mama wanted us to move to Granny's place; closer to our old life. But I'll never understand why she passed away. Did she do it on purpose? So we could miss her and wish her back? So Father could beg and say he was sorry about their fights? I'll never understand but Auntie Sara told me Mama was taken away by cancer. What's cancer? She didn't answer me. She just bent her head over her body and cried some more. Later she held Chika and I to her bosom and told us in a few words.

like Santa Claus, with his big belly, huge features and his grey beard.

"Things are different now, I have to protect you. It's my duty as a father and I will not fail God," he told me during one of his visits to my room.

One night, he pushed me against the wall. "No one will know what happened to you if you die. I'll say you killed yourself, you hear?" I started to recite Psalm 23 and thought of Mama's smile.

*He leads me through the path of righteousness for his name sake even though I walk through the valley of the...*

I heard footsteps... he was coming for me.

He smelt of garlic and spirit. I wanted to scream but I stopped myself. I bit my lips so hard to keep the tears from falling. I wanted to shout as he moaned over my fragile body, his huge stomach covered me completely and if you were watching from our roof, you would have thought Father was masturbating. I wanted to tell him to stop like I used to. I wanted to drive my sharp teeth into his thick muscles; I desperately wanted to call on someone to help. But I learnt long ago that such pleas were useless. One night, Tiger T came by the house and knocked until father was forced to open the door.

"Ermm... good evening oga."

"Ehn ehn Tiger, wetin happen?" I could hear father's distracted voice from my room.

"I thought I heard Nonso screaming so I say make I come check am."

"Nonso na your pikin? Ehn? Abi you don dey see double with the gbana wey you dey smoke. If my daughter dey cry, na me bit am because she no dey hear word."

# THE RED ROAD
## *Toyin Odewunmi*

I stayed in my room throughout the night. The rain played its familiar drum beats on our roof. I heard my friends singing outside.

*Rain, rain, go away, come again another day, little children want to play.*

They sang like those little blue birds on TV. Cheery voices rang through the thunder and hard pellets fell in buckets and bowls placed outside to collect rain water.

I curled up like a millipede and I fell asleep and dreamt of our old life.

"If you tell anyone, I'll kill you."

His eyes burnt through his skull like fire and tears flowed freely down my face. Papa was a fierce looking man. He had thick, dark brows that were barely divided at the centre of his forehead. His dark skin made it difficult to tell where the brows began and where they ended. I remember playing with his bushy beard when I was five. I thought he looked hair unwinding. Big sculpted shelves on the side of the mountain. I feel safe here   slide   turn   come down   onward   red rock and towering pines. I feel safe here.

# I FEEL SAFE HERE
*Barbara Henning*

Car windows rolled down, hair blowing and the blue sky spreading out around my shoulders. Miles of hills, grass, cattle—cattle, that's the name for herds of cows meant to be slaughtered. Around the bend a vista of mountains covered with pine trees, the road swerving down into fields of yellow grass. On the Afghan roads, grenades and explosives are casually tossed into passing cars. Two slender deer pose in the middle of the road, long legs and long necks, two together. Nice legs, honey. One of them looks over at me with her ears perked. Last year more than two-thousand one-hundred and eighteen Afghan civilians were killed. I am sitting in the car and the black SUV behind me has come to a stop, too. We've been traveling together for fifty miles or so. Two journalists kidnapped in Kandahar. Nurbidi and her lover buried to the waist and then stoned to death. The deer turn around and slowly lope back into the pines. The dervishes in Basra twirl, their long black there is only a vague space left behind, whose end and beginning is indiscernible. Finally, with a force that makes me clutch my stomach, the surgeon inserts a folded lens the size of a pinky toenail. Two spiral arms pop open and hook along the inner edge of the iris. A few movements of wetting and rearranging, and the vacuum is jerked out (my stomach lurches), and across the new eyeball flutter the wettest eyelashes, eager to reconnect. And I remember this eye is attached not only to a cheek and a body, but also to a life. I need more of a helping hand than she does as I attempt to leave; I grope the painted walls as I slowly walk out. The patient, green cup taped to her tired face, merely adjusts her hair, and leaves, only a few days from perfect vision.

# IRIS
*Iris Brilliant*

I always imagined its consistency to be that of a hardboiled egg. Perhaps I've read too much Georges Bataille or spent countless breakfasts wishing my fork upon the glaring orbits of my enemies. But one needs more than a butter knife to slice through it.

The sound of deflating bagpipes drones loudly as the surgeon penetrates the slit between blue and white. Only local anesthesia and words of comfort are used here. The patient is wide awake, feet akimbo, hands unclenched. Only in India can a stranger watch foreign eyes be penetrated, jabbed, and restored, no MD to my name, no forms to fill out, just a smile and a white face. The nurse lubricates the white while the surgeon deftly breaks apart the clouded lens, sucking up the jagged pieces into the vacuuming device. The patient hasn't flinched. Her eyelids are pinned neatly beneath her eyebrows, atop her cheeks. The vacuum whirs and chases each fragment of opaque blue, sucking them up into its bottomless mouth until and pushing forward, reached for the flaming Strat. But the guitarist shouldered him aside and grabbing its neck, smashed it down, over and over until only splintered wood and twisted metal remained. He heaved the smoking wreckage into the stunned crowd.

A thick pot-laced fog floated across the stage. Joseph sucked it in, trembling. Faces wavered and blurred. He stared at his fingers and flipped the toggle switch.

"So ya just couldn't keep your hands off it," the aging hippie said.

"Wha… what the hell?" Joseph shuddered. He clutched the P Bass and gazed at its owner. "Look, man, I was just checking the action and—"

"Yeah, yeah, that's what they all say." He grinned. "You'd better take care of that arm. Those burns look nasty. Hendrix, right?"

Joseph stared wide-eyed at his arm and nodded. "I… I just couldn't stand there while he destroyed that beautiful guitar."

"You got off easy. The last guy who messed with my bass found himself in a plane with Buddy Holly, Ritchie Valens and the Big Bopper."

Joseph touched his singed flesh gingerly, his eyes glazing. *But that fine Strat… what memories it musta held. Maybe Jimi knew he could never do better with it, so it had to go.*

The dude packed up his P Bass. "So how much do I owe ya?"

"No charge, man." Joseph waved him off, knowing what memories are really worth.

quickly and packed it in its case.

He hoisted his own worn ax from the wall rack, fingered the strings, and daydreamed about his years with rock bands touring the West Coast, that adventurous time before Lucy, a mortgage, and two hyper kids. *If I'd just stuck with it, I might have made it. Yeah, that's what everyone says… the road not taken.*

As the afternoon dragged on, curiosity ate at Joseph. He retrieved the Fender, plugged it in, and flipped the mysterious toggle switch. But the bass's sound didn't change. Joseph thumped the E-string slowly. Strange noises echoed throughout the shop, sounding like people yelling, chanting something he couldn't quite make out. The walls faded slowly to black and he stared into the darkness at a massive crowd. The air stank of reefer. Footlights and overheads lit the stage, its deck vibrating under Joseph's feet. At his back, a drummer beat the crap out of a trap set. Spotlights caught a black dude with a huge Afro wailing on a left-handed guitar. His long fingers flew over the fret board as he leaned into a Marshall amplifier, the feedback deafening. He moved to a microphone and moaned: "Hey Joe, where ya goin' with that gun in your hand." The song blasted from towering speakers.

*That can't be who I think it is… somebody musta slipped me somethin'… but it's so cool.* Joseph's fingers slid over the P Bass's strings, playing riffs he didn't remember learning. The black dude stopped his antics but the drummer increased the beat. "Jimi, I love you," some chick screamed. The crowd surged forward. The guitarist laid his beautiful psychedelic-painted Stratocaster on the stage and knelt before it, as if in prayer. He squirted lighter fluid on the ax, bent and kissed its neck, then lit it up. Joseph stared in horror straighten her up, I might need to level the frets so it doesn't buzz."

"No problem. Just don't screw with anything else." The man glared at Joseph. "I've had others mess with it and they've paid for their transgressions."

*Transgressions? What is this guy, some kinda preacher?* "Don't worry, man. I've been a luthier for ten years, fixed thousands of instruments."

"Huh. Well, just leave the electronics alone."

"No problem. I can have it ready before closing. It'll cost somewhere between forty and seventy dollars."

"Cool."

"Can I get your name and phone number?"

"No. I'll be back." The man turned and left the shop.

*What an ass, as if I could screw up a P Bass's electronics. They're so simple, a monkey could rewire 'em.*

Joseph made short work of the truss rod adjustments and replaced the worn strings. Plugging the Fender into his amplifier, he checked the intonation and played his favorite riffs. Thunderous bass notes rattled everything not glued down.

*It's perfect, no buzzes, an easy fifty bucks.* He admired the old bass's original equipment. *Now that's strange!* Joseph touched a toggle switch tucked under the chrome bridge cover and hidden from view. *Looks like some kinda phase switch... but on a Precision Bass?* He laid the Fender on the workbench and removed the cover to get a better look. The switch was mounted on a plate. Joseph unscrewed it and discovered a tiny blinking box and microprocessor connected to the switch. His mouth dropped open. *Never seen anything like this, what the hell does it do?* But remembering the hippie's warning, he reassembled the instrument

# THE LUTHIER
*Terry Sanville*

Joseph heard the door creak open and turned from his workbench. A gray-bearded man with long hair pushed into the shop, carrying a battered guitar case. *Jeez, another geezer wanting me to tell him how great his guitar is.*

"How can I help you?"

The aging hippie studied him, frowning. "I've got this P Bass that needs its neck straightened, and a set of new strings. Can ya handle it?"

"Sure, let's take a look." Joseph opened the case and stared at the electric bass guitar. *Holy moley, this thing's a '55, or maybe a '56.* He carefully lifted the heavy Fender and sighted down its neck.

"Yep, it's got a bit of a bow. But a few tweaks of the truss rod should straighten it. What kind of strings do you want?"

"The same that's on there. I can't remember the brand."

Joseph again sighted down the neck. "When I

else had he always kept them for last? I felt I owed him an apology, but I could not bring myself to say to a full-grown man with strands of gray in his beard that I was sorry, so sorry, to have eaten his piece of candy. So the months went by. Until yesterday, when I found it in my department mailbox: a Ziploc bag full of all those black jellybeans he'd saved.

# **EVIDENCE**
## *Danielle LaVaque-Manty*

I discovered Turner's habit the day we voted to hire that new guy to teach taxes and torts. He lined up five jellybeans along the edge of the conference table, spaced three inches apart: red, green, blue, white, black. Every ten minutes, he ate one. Christ, I thought, the boredom is driving him insane. But the next meeting, he did it again: red, green, blue, white, black. I mentioned it to Buchanan, who said how could I possibly not have noticed this about Turner, he's been doing it for years, eats them in the same order every time. So the next meeting, I ate the black bean. Turner blinked twice at the spot where it had been before turning his sorrowful eyes on me. He'd already eaten the red one, but he left the green, blue, and white beans sitting there the rest of the hour. On his way out, he dropped them in the trash. From then on he only brought red, green, blue, and white. It seemed I'd ruined the black ones for him forever. They'd probably been his favorites—why

"So," he says and the way he looks at me, left eyebrow arched, lips turned up at the corners, confirms my worst suspicions.

the tiled floor, careful not to let it happen again. As I focus on my mission, my left heel slips slightly, my crepe soled shoes meeting an unfriendly surface, and I emit a sigh of relief, having deflected disaster.

Pausing at the white bakery box filled with the usual assortment of delicacies, I feel as though the entire department is watching.

I gingerly pick up my preferred bit of fried dough, and set it neatly on the small, square paper napkin provided, ignoring the spots of grease appearing instantly. The only distinguishable sound, the normal buzz of people hard at work.

I clear my throat, turning my head slightly at a ringing phone, begging to be answered. When a "hello" stills the tone, I smile. Drawing in a gulp of air, I take my measured progress, eyes downcast, guaranteeing neither the doughnut nor my feet perform an action of humiliation.

Aware that the last part of any trip can be the most perilous, I am especially careful. Within inches of my armless swivel chair, the toe of my shoe appears to be stuck to the carpet. I hold my breath, clutching the napkin, hoping this tiny glitch has gone unnoticed while I gain control of the situation.

I plunk down in my seat thinking I've made a significant conquest. No one has noticed. No one cares about my awkwardness and, most importantly, no one has been laughing at me. Smiling, I take the first delicious bite of the well earned trophy only to hear throat clearing.

"Hi." Martin is standing in my doorway.

"Hi," I respond weakly, my tongue running over my upper lip eradicating any chocolate icing residue. If Martin is speaking to me, all cannot be lost. I am one with the tiny universe where I spend my days.

# **THE LAST LAUGH**
## *Janet Yung*

Not given to overt bursts of paranoia, I hadn't noticed anything unusual after the initial curiosity about the incident. That was the way I'd come to refer to the whole unfortunate episode: "the incident."

Really, in the scheme of things, no big deal and being of the firm belief I can laugh at myself as much as the next person, I didn't see a cause for alarm. But the subtle shift in mood and attitude around me began to form the basis for the nagging sensation that everyone else was finding humor in something I'd considered embarrassing. And, unlike me, they were unable to let it go.

Friday is doughnut day. Not the sort to turn down a chocolate-iced cake one, I wait until the hubbub gathered around the coffee pot has thinned out before making my move and setting off to claim mine.

I sense eyes are trained on my progress as I retrace the steps of the incident. Diligently, I mince across then another. Maybe it would come all the way up to the house.

Rick turned around and stepped from the bird's view. Then he ran to the counter and grabbed his phone, opening it to the camera. He ran back to the door, peeking through the window; the backyard was empty. He threw open the door and stepped out, thinking maybe he'd just overlooked the bird—but he could see it, in his neighbor's yard. It looked back at him and squawked once, then took off, running faster than he would've thought possible, and by the time he'd brought his phone up, the bird had disappeared around the side of the house.

Rick looked through the viewfinder on his phone for a moment, then flipped it closed and slid it into his pocket. He stood there, watching where he'd last seen the bird, then picked up the garbage, put it in the bin, and went back inside. An hour later, when Lauren called to check up on him, he didn't mention the bird, nor the discarded casserole. He smiled and laughed at one of his wife's bland jokes, then hung up the phone and watched the rest of the game.

little over three feet tall, kind of bulky but not fat. Its wings were small, tucked against its side like wilted arms. Its plumage, various shades of light and medium grays, glistened in the afternoon sun, and the bird turned its head to stare at him, its large eyes open and curious.

Rick couldn't move. The bird bobbed its head, its beak opening slightly. Its muscular legs, a dull yellow, seemed to want to take a step forward, but the bird, perhaps cautious of humans after having become extinct, stood still. Instead, it winked at him, the burnt orange eye conveying some sentiment, some shared knowledge that caused Rick to let his breath out in relief. The bird ducked its head, as if understanding, but didn't move any closer or farther away.

Rick looked around, being careful not to move his head. His yard was separated from the others by a decorative chain-link fence, and he could tell that none of his neighbors were out. He briefly wondered where the bird had come from—the nearest forest was a couple miles away, but of course that only mattered if dodos were forest birds, and who knew that—but then brought his mind back to the fact that no one else was watching the bird but him.

His camera phone was on the kitchen counter. Rick slowly set the garbage bag down on the patio, wincing as something shifted within the bag. The bird watched him, almost patiently, and it winked again, and though he figured there was no significant meaning in it, he winked back just in case.

He eased into the house, wishing he could keep the back door open. It went into place with a soft click, and he watched through the window as the bird took a small step forward, still watching him,

# DODO
*Daniel W. Davis*

Rick walked out into his backyard and there it was.

He held the garbage bag in one hand, the weight of last night's burnt casserole straining against the plastic. It was another of Lauren's failures, and when she called later that afternoon he would tell her he'd eaten it all, and she'd cook the same thing in a couple weeks, and he would go through the motions again.

With the sound of the game on in the background—the Bears were down again, but when were they not—he nudged the back door open, propping it with his foot. From there, the garbage bin was just a couple feet away, and he could throw the bag in and step back into the house and not miss a beat. It was too damn muggy to linger.

Except he did linger. He stood there and stared.

It was a dodo bird. He knew that right away, because he remembered seeing cartoon drawings of them in grade school. "D" for "Dodo." It was a three boys hear a mermaid cry, great gulping whelps and shrieks, and words they can't distinguish because they only speak English and had balked at taking a foreign language. Instead, they laugh and it comes out in party streamers of hoots and hollers decorating the air.

"Darn it," Jacks says. He is angry at the rock and at the mermaid because maybe she moved but even if she didn't, it's probably still her fault.

"My sister can throw better," laughs Henry B.

"My grandmother can, and she's blind in one eye," says Henry P.

Jacks doesn't like the jeering. The next rock hits the mermaid's back, leaving a messy artist's palette of red, black and blue.

Jacks throws another rock, hitting her arm. Her tail reacts, furiously flapping.

Jacks hits that tail, proud because it was a moving target. She spins around looking for the source. The mermaid cradles herself, trying to smooth the nicked tail back together.

While the mermaid is attempting this self-repair, Jacks says, "Come on Henrys," offering each a rock. The Henrys were imagining what their tails would look like, if they had them. Henry B.'s was scales and armor, while Henry P.'s had feathers with eyeball patterns.

"I said come on," Jacks repeats. "This is not a game. This is war."

The rocks are thrown from furious fists, imitating a machine gun's rat-a-tat-tat. They get her everywhere. Jacks leads the pack, and he makes sure the boys know the score, announcing each hit.

The sounds the mermaid makes are unlike anything they have heard. All of them have a mother, a sister or else they know someone's sister, a grandmother, a lady teacher, and a dog that had puppies. Who really knows a mermaid? Most go through a lifetime of swimming lessons and ocean vacations and country club pools and backyard sprinklers never having encountered one. And most won't. But on this day, they can't think anymore. They listen to the staccato whir of the insects, and the a cappella breathing of their own lungs.

Jacks notices it first. He stands up to pee behind a tree, mocking Henry P. that this is how a real man does it.

Then, "Shh," he says to the others who are trying to remember the words to a song. "Shut up."

"What?" the Henrys say.

"I see something," Jacks says. He thinks that at night when he's wishing for super flying powers he should be asking for extra seeing instead.

In the middle of the lake there appears to be.

"A mermaid!" Henry P. says.

She is there, the sun kissing her golden. Long ginger hair with a seaweed and pearl crown on top of her head. French vanilla face and arms. And the lower torso a fish ... blue-grey scales poised sleekly on the rocks with a swishing tail.

"I've seen fish in the grocery," Henry P. says, his eyes so wide he's afraid they may never close again. "But they're dead."

"She's so not dead," Henry B. says.

They watch with the new enthusiasm of those recognizing a great masterpiece of previously undiscovered art.

But then Jacks says, "Mermaids don't really exist."

"Well, what is it then?" asks Henry B.

"Yeah," adds Henry P.

Jacks is their leader and he likes to be listened to. "I dunno," he says with the great authority of someone who thinks he knows everything else. "But this is our lake."

The first rock is not aimed very well.

# THIS IS WAR
*Sharon Goldner*

Three boys decide to go have fun down at the lake. Shortly after they arrive, something terrible happens.

But not right away.

Right away they float and swim, splash and push each other in.

Jacks, Henry B. and Henry P.

When they are done, because even a good time has a shelf date, they dry themselves off. They wish they brought drinks because all that fun has made their tongues dry. They would have sipped the lake water, but Henry P. thinks maybe he did exactly that: peed in between swimming strokes.

They call him an idiot, and he says, "You guys would have done the same thing," and they agree. So they each let the spit collect in their mouths, and swallow that instead. They try to forget their thirst by talking sports, favorite foods, and what's in a girl's diary. Soon, their words drift into the humid air, and

He wishes he could command them to fold their wings boat-like against their bodies, find her by smell or sound, bite their way through every screen, every crack in the brick, wood, plaster of where she is, and after hemorrhaging her of every drop of her blood, sail up her twat, and break all its teeth.

# A TRAVELER IN WINTER
*Faye Kicknosway*

While he, jape, dupe, frog prince in shiny pants and comic nose, did a pratfall off his lily pad, his valentine, his tit of honey, from the stew she cooked, the dress she hemmed, the curtains she hung, the drain she cleared with the plunger, conjured up a hardware clerk, a stock broker, an insurance salesman, commanding each to carry her off, every shoe, every piece of underwear.

May their teeth rot and they go blind and fall off roofs and get strangled in kite strings, and eaten by bears, or better yet get slowly and painfully killed by the ravenous offspring of small Amazonian fish that swim up a stream of urine and attach their eggs inside the dick pissing it.

There's a hole in the bedroom screen the size of Nebraska and he thinks he'll grab a six pack, fill the tub with cold water and every ice cube in the fridge, and escape the wheezing in the air he knows must be every mosquito on the North American continent.

thin abdomen. So, I get the black light. Yes, I have one. I had five years to buy the thing. I hold it up to him. He's, wow, he's human. Not bad looking at all. Green shirt, blue pants, big green eyes, blond hair. A little thin, but big chest. A genius size head. His clothes look a little like Gainsborough's Blue Boy, but maybe this ancient creature does not know how to dress for the twenty-first century. He looks quite a bit like that darned fairy did.

So this is it. I have my scalpel in hand. I get ready to go for his wings.

Something stops me. Maybe it's just the time of morning which softens the edges. Maybe it's the fact I was up all night and am a little fuzzy. Maybe it's his eating habits. Maybe I want to stay single.

I carry him to the front of the house and toss him into the air. I watch him do a couple of loops and backflips around my head. Then he is gone beyond the oranges and purples of the sunrise of my eighteenth birthday.

I nodded stupidly, my next question on my lips as she flew away. "What do I feed him?" "Well," I thought. "That fairy certainly seems to be in a hurry!"

Dragonfly nymphs are the ugliest, most predatory insect sharks in the lake. Probably the world. After my little blue-green fairy flew away I took my jar and scooped up a tubular brown animal the length of a centimeter. It had a wormlike body, huge eyes, and as I was to learn, a distendible jaw or prementum. I was to spend the next five years of my life collecting insect larvae and other little wiggles to feed him. I watched, first in horror, then in disgusted fascination as my ancient trilobite with water jets used his spiky jaws to grab, dismantle shell, tear flesh, suck, bite and gulp his way to large dragonfly size. Not exactly a romantic dating period. I threw in everything alive and he ate it. He did not hesitate to eat other nymphs, the cannibal.

As my boyfriend got larger and fatter, I needed a bigger space for him, so he ended up in a five-gallon aquarium. He did not hesitate to eat small fish. Or worms. Or tadpoles. He ate them all.

It's just about time. My creature has climbed out of the aquarium and is sitting on the rim. It's sunset in springtime. We did have a swine plague. There are still some boys and men left, but not too many. Of course there were never too many in this podunk town of Atascadero. The light is coming in from the curtains to the west. I watch in silence while Mr. Darner dries off, splits his skin and starts to pump blood into his wings. This, unlike muscle flexing, is not at all sexy, but it's beautiful in a weird way. By morning I am faced with an insect of incredible beauty, with huge green eyes, green thorax and blue beautiful face... blond hair... green eyes. She was about a hand long, a hand with long fingernails.

"Well sweetie, we're reaching the end of society as we know it," she said as she looped around my head, doing backflips.

"What are you talking about?" I said, trying to take a picture. She wouldn't let me.

"There's gonna be a big flu epidemic spread by pigs. Most of the males of your species will either die or become sterile. So if you want to get married and have kids, you and I'd better talk about it now."

"How is this going to happen?" I wondered aloud.

"I don't know. Something about the lack of resistance from the Y chromosome. Give me a break. This may be the twenty-first century, and I have magic, but I'm no scientist." Her melodious voice sounded slightly peeved. "So, honey, if you want a husband, here's what you have to do. See those big green and blue dragonflies, the Green Darners? Go catch one of their nymphs and feed it for five years. They can last that long. Then you'll be eighteen and ready to mate. As soon as it becomes an adult, pull off his wings, and you'll have a strapping fertile man."

"Just like that?" I stammered.

"Well I don't have all day. However, I can answer one or two questions."

"How will I know if it's the right nymph? Can I see what he looks like first?"

"Teenagers," she muttered. "Don't worry, you'll find the right nymph. Green Darners are very common, and frankly, this is magic. As for inspecting the merchandise before making a commitment, just put him under a black light. You do know what that is, right?"

# **FAIRY TAIL**

## (for ann cooper)
### *Diane Klammer*

I'm keeping my future husband in a five-gallon aquarium. Actually, he started out in a jar. Then he graduated to the fish bowl. This is the end of a five year long process. When he metamorphoses, he'll turn into a human. Or, I'll get to turn him into a human.

I'm about to turn eighteen. When I was thirteen, I was at the lake in the back of our house, looking at dragonflies. I loved to play by the lake on a warm summer day in Atascadero and watch all the creatures hanging around. I would catch miniature trout and little invertebrates in a jar. I loved all the frogs and turtles, the sunsets, the birds.

One day a fairy flew up to me. She said, "Yes darling, I'm a fairy. I know it's the twenty-first century, but we still exist. Close your mouth, you'll get a fly in it." She wore a green blouse and blue skirt and had gorgeous lacy green wings. She had a

Now Donny really isn't in the market for a wife on this beautiful Saturday in plastic world, but he's never seen anyone as beautiful as Marie in his whole life. As one woman after another is bid on and married away to the mall-visiting man of her dreams, Donny can't stop looking at his Marie. He approaches the stage, starry-eyed. He bids. He wins.

Marie is shy, demure behind that perpetual toothy smile. Like any bride wife who has just been sold from a platform in the middle of a shopping mall, she is nervous. She approaches the edge of the stage as if she is entering civilization for the first time. She shyly accepts Donny's hand and steps from the platform, scared like a little bird. The few onlookers applaud the new married couple.

Donny, now manly and confident, leads his new wife away from the auctioning block, away from the platform and the mall to his shoebox Ferrari. A short drive across the carpet later the newlyweds arrive home. Marie is again overwhelmed, as she's apparently never seen a house before, and Donny shows her the two plastic fold-up walls ending at the bedroom, which, ironically, is the only room in this cheap, non-Barbie brand plastic house. In the fold-out plastic bed they kiss, him the sweet but firm aggressor, her compliant, and then finally they are naked, her plastic legs swiveled out, his nondescript bulge pushing between.

The plot never went any further. By then the game had reached its shaky conclusion, the sky was darkening and my mother was calling me to dinner.

# DONNY AND MARIE OSMOND BARBIE
*Nancy Stohlman*

My Donny and Marie Osmond Barbie dolls came with matching purple outfits—Donny had purple socks that slipped into white shoes, and both Donny and Marie had holes drilled through their left hands for their matching microphones that I promptly lost. Their brunette heads were fastened onto typical Barbie bodies, Marie's 38—22—26, feet permanently arched for high-heels, Donny's nondescript bulge.

There was only one game I played with Donny and Marie Osmond Barbie, who were no longer brother and sister. It went like this: Donny wakes one morning ready for another exciting day in plastic world. After a refreshing plastic breakfast, he decides to go to the mall. In the atrium of the mall an event is happening, a large, raised platform with a line of beautiful women, including Marie. It's a Wife Auction—the fast-talking announcer is rattling off his prizes to the highest bidder.

me, and I never had to eat alone while Eric ate in another room adjacent to the office lobby. I never left the cool autumn comfort of the Legion Hall's concrete. In this story, I make it so it's like it never happened, not one bit. And not just the suspension. I am beyond the suspension now. I am older, sitting on the steps outside my house, in front of the door from which my father calmly called to me years earlier. A car pulls up, my friends exit. Cheers rise up in the distance from the Friday night football game at the high school a couple of blocks away. My friends let me cry because my father has died, and I do it, because I don't think I could have otherwise. I think I needed their permission. But I am beyond that now. I am older, sitting, typing, still wishing it away.

In the real story, the world falls away over and over, breaks apart beneath every footstep, like it was always waiting for me to walk there. In the real story, people died, and I had to admit I bit someone. In this story, none of that happens.

I am still sitting on the concrete in front of the Legion Hall. It's cool. So is the breeze that wanders down the street slowly and drunkenly, herding leaves and kicking an empty cup across the asphalt. My head drags itself across the pine siding of the Hall, making a crackling noise that reverberates in my head wonderfully, one of those little sounds only you can hear, like chewing a carrot with your ears plugged, or dunking your head in a warm bath, submerging your ears, and humming. Above the soft crackle, I hear my father call to me, asking if everything is okay. I can hear the concern in his voice, the love. But I don't get up in this story. I stay there across the street, and just burst into flames.

suspended from school. It will be an in-school suspension, meaning I will have to sit for two days on an uncomfortable, over-sprung, brown Naugahyde bench. I will have to do my homework there, take my lunch there, and be humiliated each time someone I know enters. I will have to answer the one question each and everyone will ask: What did you do? This is the reason the Legion Hall seems so nice, so comforting, so womb-like—it gives me a certain solace from home. See, I am not afraid of telling my father that I was suspended, that's child's play in comparison to the task of relating why: I have been suspended from school, at the age of fourteen, for biting Theresa Mills.

Yes, biting, and no, her real name was not Theresa.

My suspension will be spent with my friend Eric who was suspended for stabbing Karen Fuchs in the forearm with a pencil to "see what, exactly, would happen."

I bit Theresa because she closed my locker, and spun the combination. I felt that the most reasonable reaction, at the time, would be to bite her on the shoulder and break the skin.

I am sitting on the concrete outside the Legion Hall, across from my house, head sanding white stained pine. In the real story, my father sees me through the wide picture window of our house and calls gently across the lawn, asking if everything is okay. In the real story, I have to face my humiliation and my father's disappointment, and two days of eating lunch in the office with a red plastic tray balanced on my knees. In the real story, I feel pathetic. But this isn't the real story, I never intended to tell it, and so my father never felt disappointed in

# **NEVER INTENDED**
## *Charles Rutter*

I am fourteen, sitting across the street from my house in Illinois, my back resting against the Legion Hall. It's painted red in places, with white siding covering the façade. An American flag falls limply against the flagpole. School buses from the garage next door rumble into bays, the last of their daily loads delivered. A 21-gun salute occurs here each Veterans Day, and scares the hell out of my dog when we happen to be outside, up the street she'll run, as far as she can, a small trail of piss following, like a leaky radiator. But my dog never really peed. Run, yes; pee, no.

I am sitting on the concrete outside the Legion Hall, slowly sanding the white siding with the back of my head, dragging it right, then left, listening to the soft crackle my hair makes against the ripples in the pine. I am trying to find the best way to tell my father, who I know is home from work and no more than two hundred feet away, that I have been recognized that it was his fate, after all, to be his own father's son and that perhaps his own son, stroking his chin now, perhaps he was the result of his father's father's daydream, that one consequence came hard upon something that emerged long ago, unplanned, in a moment meant for avoiding fear.

Flying over the city when he was a boy, the man had planted a home and drawn the thick line and put the girl inside the house. He had drawn this girl. He had guaranteed his own child's future. With all his heart he'd drawn a world, and here was his son with a girl born when the man was a boy inside a plane passing high above the surrounding landscape.

Nothing came out of the father's mouth—not even when he found his face pressed into the carpet, his son turning his body over and the girl crying so hard her tears fell on the man's face.

The son sped into the foyer to call 911, and the father was left alone with his creation.

The girl tried to reassure him, her long hair scratching his face, her colorless mouth curving into a smile she must have hoped would comfort him. You're not alone, she said to the father. I'm here.

The paramedics were late finding their way over the snowy country roads.

smeared lenses he could see little, although he sensed something was wrong. He put out his hand. The girl's palm was light as a whisper. Into the house the father followed his son and the girl, their footsteps echoing.

Almost imperceptibly, the floor slanted. The man felt as if he'd been drinking.

In the nearly empty living room he stopped, amazed. He made his way to a couch, the cushions thick and squishy looking. Everything was out of plumb—as if the house had been built by a do-it-yourselfer.

The girl's high voice came from a long way away.

She was thin, and her chin was lopsided. The man nodded at her, hoping he might look friendly. He was thinking of his own wife in heaven, how he was forgetting her, part by part. Nevertheless, he could still recall her yeasty fullness, her thick waist he had liked to put an arm around. Every year in photographs she looked younger. Now this girl—already faded. He could not stop staring at her, even when she set before him and his son a tray of cookies that were powdered with dots.

The man folded his hands on his lap. He made himself look at his son, who stroked his chin and smiled.

The father did not know what to say—as if his mind had created an illusion.

"You look pale."

The father opened his mouth to respond to the voice coming from somewhere above him. With all his heart, he wanted his son to choose his own life. A life his son made for himself. But perhaps it was inevitable—a father makes a son with every breath he breathes. In his amazement, his shame, the man

How odd a city looks from the air. There's nothing to compare it to except circuitry or metal studs on blue jeans or chains that have been flung from a height. When the stewardess returned the boy was so engrossed he didn't answer her. She drew back, smiling, checking his seat belt and believing she had staunched the flood of one child's misery.

The man's memory comforted him, but within minutes after staring into his son's open face, he could not stop a sensation of hollowness from rolling in his abdomen. All his life he had been tumbling down a hill and now he had nearly reached the bottom. He told himself that he should find solace in the fact that a daughter-in-law would enter the family. Perhaps she and his son would have a child.

"Don't be nervous," the son said once they were in the rental car.

The heater in the car hardly worked. The man flexed his hands and wished he had worn gloves.

They were in farming country. Black fences. White snowy hills. Even the spruces were black-looking. More and more fences were laid like grids over the white distance.

When the car stopped, the son's face was alive with anticipation.

Snow had fallen heavily. It was early evening, and the father could hardly breathe. He stepped out of the car, the ground crackling under his shoes.

The girl who was to be his daughter-in-law must have heard them drive up, for the door of the house was instantly flung open. The son engulfed a slight form in his arms.

The man took off his glasses to brush away flakes of snow. The son thrust his father forward. Panicking, the father put his glasses on. Through the

# DRAWN FROM LIFE
## *Lee Upton*

The plane was on its descent when the father endured a terrible sense of familiarity. He tried to settle his mind by looking at the city below him, its starkness in the sunlight, the highways cutting through the landscape. His son punched his arm, and the man turned to see his wonderful smile.

Just then the man recalled his first trip by plane when he was a little fellow flying alone to see his grandmother. The stewardess, seeing his effort not to cry, found paper for him and a pencil. She stooped. You're not alone, she said. I'm here. Why don't you draw what you see outside your window?

He took it as a command.

He felt a chill when he took the pencil, for it was wet looking as if used to stir a drink. He drew clouds from outside his window or what he thought clouds should look like, big huffing puffs. He drew the land around the city that the plane was passing over and a house and a few other things.

Janata gets to it, while the rest of us continue to beat these goddamned effigies, well into the nervous angels of another dead crayon colored night.

were make believe placed there when the two of them were in a basement or something, behind locked doors, where God intended people to kiss one another in the first place."

"Good." Prakash is visibly relieved. "I don't know what we'd have done if the effigy that we're burning of Richard Gere for kissing a woman in public was itself kissed in public by a woman. Shit. We'd have to also start burning effigies of the effigy, and that could get weird."

"Do you have your stick?"

I tell Prakash that I do.

"Let's do this then." And with that he lights my Richard Gere effigy on fire.

"Go to hell grope fucker!" Prakash screams, striking the first blow with his own stick against the side of the now flaming effigy's head.

"Yes. What Prakash said!" I scream, striking the effigy in what would be its scrotal area if it had nuts.

As I continue to beat the Richard Gere effigy I can see Prakash. He seems pleased, until he notices the effigy that Janata is attempting to set fire to behind me.

"Wait!" Prakash screams as he storms towards Janata.

They're behind me now, so I can't see them. I can hear Prakash though, scolding Janata in that way that Prakash does.

"What the fuck do you have against Matthew "McConahey?!" Prakash asks Janata.

"Nothing Prakash," Janata assures him.

"Then why the hell does your effigy look like Matthew McConahey? We are not burning Matthew McConahey today! We're burning Richard Gere! Now get to it!"

Lewis that he played in the movie *Pretty Woman* in effigy. It's not the character of Edward Lewis who has disgraced us. It is the actor who portrayed Edward Lewis that we have the intolerable beef with. Write something like 'This effigy is Richard Gere, not Edward Lewis' across his forehead or something. In this way we will be clear."

I do as Prakash instructs. As I'm doing this he notices the marker'd lipstick marks that I'd previously added to the side of its face.

"What is that?" Prakash asks.

"Those are meant to be lipstick marks, placed there in pretend earlier days by the infidel's on-screen movie partner, the lovely Julia Roberts."

Prakash thinks about this for a couple of seconds.

"You say lovely? Do you really mean lovely? Do you not instead think that this Julia Roberts has a face that looks like a Bambi which has been crossed with a horse?"

"Yes Prakash, you are right. I meant to say horse face."

"Doe-eyed horse face."

"Yes. Doe-eyed horse face."

Together we laugh.

Then Prakash stiffens as if he's just thought of something, because he has.

"These lipstick marks that you've placed on the cheek of your Richard Gere effigy, they were not make-believe placed there by the lips of Julia Roberts while your effigy and this pretend Julia Roberts were in public, were they?"

Holy shit! Why the hell didn't I think about that?

"No Prakash," I assure him. "These lip marks

now as it has been made.

"Make it look like he did in *Pretty Woman*!"

Prakash barks some other orders to his brother Bharatiya and then goes back to beating his own effigy of Richard Gere with a stick.

"Die Public Lip Kisser!" I hear Prakash scream, his stick striking the life sized figure made from farm straw and borrowed pillow cases that is meant to represent the actual body of the American thespian heathen. Sparks shoot far into the sky as I look around to find that I am almost the only one involved in this angry mob who has not yet lit my own Richard Gere effigy on fire and proceeded to beat the flaming crap out of it with a stick.

Quickly I take the magic marker that I have recently inherited from my father and attempt to smug up my Richard Gere's facial expression by shading a little extra smirkyness around his lips. Also I fix its hairstyle. And as an additional touch, one which it turns out that I am extremely proud of and came to me in an inspired rush, I add what is supposed to be lipstick marks on the side of his face. Then I get Prakash.

"I am finished," I tell him.

Prakash is sweating and breathing heavily. He inspects my effigy carefully with a zealous glaze that has covered his eyes.

"That's better," Prakash tells me. "Yes. I like what you've done to the nose as well. It's nice and big."

"Thank you Prakash," I tell him, attempting to hide the new pride.

"Yes, you have captured the character of Edward Lewis quite well," Prakash says this, then he pauses. "Perhaps too well. We don't want to confuse anyone into thinking we're burning the character Edward

# **RICHARD GERE EFFIGY**
## *Rob Geisen*

"How the fuck am I supposed to burn this? It looks nothing like him!"

Prakash is displeased with me. We're burning effigies of the American actor Richard Gere on account of he kissed a woman several times in public at a recent AIDS awareness event. Prakash says such displays of public affection are forbidden.

"They are gross and disgusting," Prakash rages. "And besides that it's taboo."

Prakash is displeased with me because he believes that the effigy I've just built for the purpose of burning does not closely enough resemble the likeness of the real-life Richard Gere. I've tried to explain to Prakash that I was attempting to capture his image as he appeared in the film *Doctor T and the Women*, but Prakash says this is bullshit. He insists nobody's seen *Doctor T and the Women* and will not understand what we are burning if we set fire to this thing that I have made here, if we set fire to it right

"To cash!"

"To phosphorous!"

Shielding her eyes from the sun, Anna watches until the blimp becomes a tiny speck against the acrid September sky.

# WAKE UP WITH ME IN THE RADISSON
*Dawn Sueoka*

Everything about the room is symmetrical. A double bed with Egyptian cotton sheets, and next to it, another one. Beside each bed is a nightstand with two putty-colored earplugs on it, and beside each nightstand is a wall-length mirror. In one of the beds, a pregnant woman sleeps. Her rarefied breathing is indistinguishable from the soft whirr of the air conditioner's motor. Anna briefly rests her hand on the woman's bare shoulder then takes one pair of earplugs from the table and goes out on the balcony. It is hot. She rolls the putty-colored foam between her thumb and forefinger and inserts first one, and then the other, into her ears. The foam quietly expands. A hundred yards away, the Goodyear blimp is ascending, and in its passenger compartment, Johnny Depp, Ronald Reagan, and Harrison Ford are raising glasses of ginger beer.

"To love!"

car" as he tore off her clothes.

At first I was haunted by the image of her—hurt and helpless, naked and afraid—and of course I wanted to kill him, the murderous man who could do such horrific things. Naturally, I knew he was most at fault and wanted to hurt him, to break him, to feel his bones crunch under my boot, but I also realized that he was, of course, crazy. There will always be crazy people in the city, weeds in the sidewalk that need to be ripped out by the roots.

But, how could a bunch of bystanders, how could ordinary people sit by and watch, and laugh even, especially another woman? This question has come to horrify me and make my stomach churn, even more than thinking about the deed itself.

Now, every time I find myself stopped in traffic I can see the faces of the on-looking bystanders refusing to help, watching her from their comfortable cars as she is beaten and abused. I see them trying to hide in the innocence of inaction, but I can smell their stinking guilt going unpunished.

I'm stopped in traffic now, near the middle of the bridge, and I can see her apparition out in the street. The cowards in the cars beside me are doing nothing. I can't believe they are going to just watch and let this happen. Look, the lady beside me is smiling, laughing even. I think she is actually cheering him on. The bastards! The monsters! I will make them pay.

I'm out of my car now. I'm going to do something. I'm going to start with her, the laughing one. The car jack from my trunk is already in my hand.

# **ROAD RAGE**
*Corey Lee Lewis*

I first read about her in the newspaper, or at least, I think I did. As I recall, I was reading the article over breakfast, and it unnerved, in fact, horrified me so much, that eggs over-easy have turned my stomach ever since.

At first, I started seeing her ghostly image on the edge of my headlights at night, but then it began happening during the day. I kept seeing her everywhere I went: stripped to her underclothes, bleeding, crying, beaten, poised on the edge of the Golden Gate Bridge, ready to jump, to escape, to flee, her attacker behind her, coming on, getting closer, with the large black car jack in his hand.

Now, I see her on every bridge I drive over, standing helpless by the railing, afraid and alone. A moment later I see her sailing, free-falling, escaping to death and oblivion below.

The newspaper said other motorists watched as he hit her, that they yelled things like "do her on the

"The guy's name was—is—Stan Wan. He's a big sexy Chinese guy, yes with that kind of gelled hair—a college student, friend of a friend of a friend. That sort of thing."

"I don't have to know."

"Yeah, you do," she said. "You'll like it. I just realized it. 'S. Wan.' Get it? And I'm Melitta—or, as my mother says, 'Lita.' It's too funny."

"Jesus," I said. "You're right. I'll never be able to read Yeats again."

"I'm so happy I have you!" she said suddenly. "You'll wait with me, won't you?"

I agreed, of course I would.

"*Waiting for Godot*," she said. "They depended on each other."

I was fourteen years older. "Anyway, it's 'above the staggering girl.' The poem."

"Is it?" She laughed. "Jeez. That's true, too. I was *staggering* the first time, at that party. The second and third times I knew exactly what I was doing."

"You counted?" I hadn't asked her, when she confided, what had happened. It was true I pictured something like a rape—at least insistence. And resistance.

"End of count." She sank back, folded into herself in defeat. "He dropped me." The gelled-hair guy in the adjacent car smacked his lips at Melitta. She pushed her middle finger in the air.

"Brazen," I said. "I couldn't have done that."

"Street smarts," she said. "He taught me a few."

"He."

"He who we're getting rid of—partially—right now. *Whom*?"

"Whom."

A car in front of us insinuated itself into another lane and we moved beyond the boom-boom. "I think I'm smarter now," she said.

"You are smart. You're the smartest sixteen-year old I've ever met," I said.

"But smart in a different way." She shook some more, shuddered in fact.

"You'll be okay. It'll be over soon."

"It's awful."

We were finally at the toll, at the metering lights, lanes were moving smoothly within our sights.

"Here's the really funny thing—I just thought of it," she said, curling under a leg, girlishly. "I can tell you."

I listened, afraid she'd change her mind, craving the confidence.

above which his square head with its dark gelled hair beat out rhythms with chin thrusts. I pictured him picking up a girl in a tight jersey somewhere in the Mission, a girl with bra straps showing, who would find him tremendously sexy. He was sexy in a way. He turned toward my stare and gave me a look I had seen in students: a challenging *What?* as in *What the hell is wrong with you?*

"Was he handsome like that?" I asked. "Your guy?"

Melitta was my student, or more specifically, my T.A. She got academic credit for recording grades in my roll book and sorting my handouts into file folders in my high school English classes. Mostly she was a sponge, absorbing everything that went on: memorizing the "To be or not to be" soliloquy with the students, arguing about Oedipus's fate, helping to direct classroom scenes from *Waiting for Godot*.

"Sort of," she said. "My 'guy.'" She gave a little gasping laugh, like a choke. "Was that a 'snigger' or a 'chortle?'"

"'Chortle' is a Lewis Carroll made-up word."

"He made it up? In *Alice*? Neat." For a moment she seemed to forget, then she remembered. "Some wonderland."

We surveyed the cars, gleaming like cheap jewels; we were in tandem with the vibrating car inching along, *ba-boom, ba-boom, ba-boom*.

Melitta slid her hands under her knees, bounced her legs nervously.

"You'll be okay."

"My parents can't know."

"It's a clinic. They're confidential."

We were quiet for a while. I loved Melitta; I loved the fact that she saw me as a sister, a mother.

# LESSONS
## *Jackie Davis-Martin*

"A sudden blow, the great wings beating still." Melitta made a little hurricane gesture with her right hand, sucked in her breath.

"What?" I said, my head turned completely from the windshield. We weren't going anywhere, the traffic at the Bay Bridge toll plaza an expanse of thirty solid lanes funneling through fourteen metering booths.

"Above the trembling girl," she said, trembling.

"Stop it," I said.

"I can't." She trembled more to prove her point. "I'm a nervous wreck."

"You've made yourself one," I offered, but my voice was drowned out by a mega speaker in an adjacent vehicle—not even a large one, although it boomed and vibrated us like a giant dentist's drill under the earth. "Christ. What is he thinking?"

The guy in the car—a souped-up Chevy or something with chrome wheels—had large shoulders

Her mother's blood saved the girl, and afterwards she found help: group therapy, psychiatrists, inpatient facilities. And years later the girl was happy and plump, tattoos of butterflies over each of her scars: a Cranberry Blue on her left—*Vacciniina optilete*—a Mourning Cloak on her right—*Nymphalis antiopa*—the raised and jagged cut marks hidden in the veins of blue and black wings, imperceptible to all but the two who know them best.

But the single mother of one saved the photos from the hidden folder she found in the program files of the family computer, and she kept them as reminders—reverse triggers, things to be happy for—changing only the file names, replacing the churlish weights with random letters: *asjkl. jkljp. dsagdu. tyadsj. risjdf. iosdgj.*

*Lunch:*
*Sugarless gum—half a pack. Jello—two cups. Skimmed milk. Frosting from one cupcake.*

*Breakfast:*
*Four cigarettes. No coffee. Half bag Doritos.*

She read on, finding other entries graphing weight changes, expressing the "geeniusness" of eating ice cubes and lollypops for dinner, and quoting the morbidly misunderstood conceptions of history's finest:

*"We never repent of having eaten too little."*
Jefferson

*"Things sweet to taste prove in digestion sour."*
Shakespeare

*"Quod me nutrit me destruit" (What nourishes me destroys me)*
Angelina Jolie

The woman realized then how little she knew her daughter. She confronted the girl, who denied and cried and retreated to the bathroom to calm her nerves in bubble bath—and later, when her mother returned to try again, failed to answer from behind the bathroom door. The woman assumed the worst, popped the lock with a bobby pin, and found her daughter in the tub, wrists sliced with a bread knife and sticky with blood. She pulled her out through the hot and pink bubbles to find that her daughter was fully dressed—a hooded sweatshirt and jeans, the cotton waterlogged and steaming—and that she was several pints lighter.

# **REVERSE TRIGGERS**
## *Matt Siegel*

A woman who long ago lived below us, a single mother of one, once found an unfamiliar folder hidden away in the program files of her family computer. Inside were photos of her daughter, arranged and labeled by weight—*111 lbs., 104 lbs., 92 lbs.*—along with assorted pictures of runway celebrities collected from entertainment sites and before-and-after photos of other teens, friends the girl made through online *thinspiration* forums and chat rooms, labeled as low as *63 lbs*. And there were other images—reverse triggers, her daughter called them—of pregnant women and the grossly obese.

After, when she searched her daughter's room, she found the jars of vomit in the closet, the diet pills in the drawer, and the misspelled entries in her daughter's diary journaling her food intake:

*Breakfast:*
*Three cigarettes. Two cups coffee. Water.*

frantic. He stares at Swathi, wills her to turn and see him smile, one quick and reassuring grin. He tries with his eyes to tickle the back of her ear, to grab her attention without words, until at last she shifts a bit, glances over her shoulder. Rodman smiles, feels his insides tighten, unable to breathe until she looks— but her eyes don't quite make it to him. Her head turns forward and goes still, and then she dives back into the test, rechecking what she has already done.

Rodman feels the air, the light, his vision of the future, all of it slip away in a flash, like price tags torn from a new shirt in one quick jerk. He stares down at his own sheet, sees what he has done so far. His forehead furrows and he feels a gasp in his throat—it wants to suck him back in, the worry and second-guessing and itch to change. It's just him and the test, now. He shakes his head, glances up without seeing, and then turns back. He darkens the round edges of his answers and moves on.

Swathi Malhotra, that's their valedictorian. He catches sight of her, several rows over and a little ahead of him so that he can see only the side of her face, the curve of her ear, a row of dark skinny fingers drumming disastrously on her cheek. It's something he's seen before, many times. Her profile working frantically through exam questions, desperate to answer right, even when she ought to know, she has to know, there's no way she'll be wrong. It's as though she thinks each test is predicting her future. The closest Rodman has ever come to this panic is with girls—on dates in dark movie theaters, lying in the bed of his pickup truck at the end of a deserted road, locked inside the master bedroom at a secret weekend kegger. He was there with Swathi, not long ago, deeply pressed into a large, canopied bed and there, really *there*, the nervousness on their faces the same, until at the last possible moment she told him, *No, wait.*

He catches a loud sucking-in of air between lips. It's Swathi, filling a final bubble and finishing early. She shuts the thin paper test booklet and folds her hands. Rodman wonders what future she's pulling out of this, the questions and answers. She will be in a white lab coat, altering and creating and healing, or she'll be in business suits, shaking hands and promising, dealing, changing. Then he imagines his own future pooling and spilling out of the answer bubbles—he is just a normal, patient man, a nobody, but he's right beside Swathi or some woman like her, working to comfort and help her past every *no, wait* she comes up against. He sees this future self so clearly that he suddenly wants more than anything to wrap that girl up inside him until everything for her is absolutely, perfectly easy, without doubt, no longer

# **THE FAILURE**
## *Marvin Shackelford*

Rodman knows the answers; at least, he sees them, lined up beside bubbles and extending, it almost seems, into a sunset somewhere off the page. It's just a matter of picking. Across the classroom, he knows the chess club kids and Dungeons & Dragons geeks, computer nerds and the high school valedictorian, they're all sucking in their breath, answering hesitantly even if they know without a doubt the difference between *Petunia* and *Patagonia*. Only one answer can be right. It's just what they do to rattle nerves. They create doubt by supplying both right and wrong instead of simply, mercifully, asking for an answer without fear of failure, without offering alternatives to what a body already knows or doesn't know. Rodman isn't prey to these traps, though; he reads the question, he feels through the answers with a light tap of his pencil's tip, and he fills a bubble with a smear of lead. He picks what sounds good. Then he moves on.

artist who agrees to sell his soul in exchange for a reliable position. $400 a week, and some benefits.

# THE UNDERSTUDY
*Katharyn Grant*

Living up in the air, like those famous acrobats whose feet never touch the ground, he had perfected anticipation, raised anxiety to high art. It was a job like any other, he told himself: $400 a week, some benefits. But after several faithful years of unrewarded waiting, he grew lazy. He no longer attended rehearsals. Lines were memorized haphazardly.

The thesaurus says that desperation and hopelessness are synonymous. But to be truly desperate one must have hope. That is the art of the understudy. He made a profession of waiting, committing dialog to the brain like sand wasted on the desert.

He knows that one day it will happen. Inevitable. A cold, flu, a death in the family. No one can escape these scenarios forever.

One day, at the last minute he will be asked to go on stage. Ill-prepared, still drunk from the night before, it could happen at any time without warning.

There is nothing sadder than an idealistic young

just out there and gone. Down inside me stirs that feeling I think we all have as kids, to get away and go somewhere bigger. I imagine myself there beside him, maybe in a long black coat, headed somewhere late at night, people I don't know waiting for me to get there. Friends everywhere. Some new thing every step further I take. I'm maybe even somebody else. A different person translated from who I've been before, fuller and brighter and somehow better, plain and in view for anyone that wants to see.

Then Mammaw's talking again. She wants to know about me, now. What I'm doing. Where I've been. What about that girl, Rachael, whom I keep reminding her left me years ago. I don't have to rush off, do I? It's late in the day. It's just me sitting there with her, house stuffy and growing dark. I'm not going anywhere.

thumb through. His face looms out of each shot like I remember from when we were kids. Dark and that wide-eyed kind of goofy. Only now his hair stands up in spikes and he's got one of those pencil-thin, sort of pointy goatees around his lips that just screams *douche bag*. Like if you've got daughters you better watch them and they better watch themselves.

"He's in what they call an abstract. They talk and carry on and it's very surreal. At the end it's very innovating. They sing a song from ancient England."

She talks on. I can tell she has no idea what she's saying, she's just parroting things my aunt's told her, but that's fine. It's the perfect soundtrack for his life. I remember him in high school, girls waxing his eyebrows during lunch, then moving north in stages, taking great giant steps. College in Greensboro, more college in Charlottesville, then he was waiting tables in New York and acting. He started talking about leaving town almost before I can remember, charming people with a grin and a jingle of words. Mammaw starts repeating some of the lines he'll be performing, all nonsense but just perfect all the same. His whole life is a progression of put-ons.

I flip through the pictures, though, past one of him and his friends, him in a long blonde wig, him and a skinny coughing girl, and I see him in the background of a shot of some other guy yanking a shirt over his head. Nick sits in an empty subway car, shadowed yellow and dark, looking off to the side. It's the one time in all these photos, in profile, that he doesn't realize the camera's on him. He's quiet and dashing through the night, content, he's right at home. He's off in the city, away from family and all the pieces of life we grew up fitting together, he's

# **STAGES**
*Marvin Shackelford*

We sit in the stuffy living room and Mammaw tells me all about her other grandson Nick. My cousin. He's appearing, she says, in a show Off Broadway. Her voice crackles excitedly beneath the hum of her window air-conditioner. I start thinking I might smother to death. I used to sell these units, go door to door like an old-timey salesman and install them. Then it got to where I just worked maintenance on them, turning screws inside and replacing components. Sometimes I'd come in when they caught fire, maybe burned out the window frame. I'd offer to replace them, service charge only. I know all the fumes they can let out. But hers just stirs the hot air, barely cooling. She's an old woman and likes it just fine.

"Here, look," she says. "Pictures his mother brought me off the computer."

Mammaw passes over a stack of glossy photos. Her hands shake and have a hard time letting go. I the butt into the fire. A whirlpool of light brightened and coalesced, then the sky opened.

*It kind of looks like a vagina*, Uncle Silas thought absently. *Just like one of those Georgia O'Keefe paintings.* The great vagina in the sky gave birth to a circle of lights. They spun and descended. *It was a genuine flying saucer!* Uncle Silas fingered his goatee in astonishment.

"Holy… Guys!" he yelled at the house, waving. He could see the back of a child's head—the child was playing a video game. The dancing news updates from twenty-four-hour cable news channels flashed from Karl and Jesse's window. "Guys!" The saucer was descending. It probed the grassy field with a livid blue searchlight.

"Aw, fuck it!" he said, and walked down the slope into the field. His hair was standing up in the back, and his stomach felt light and fluttery, but he just kept thinking the same thought over and over again: *This is it. It will never happen again. Not like this. This is a once in a lifetime opportunity, to find out if all that crap Donnie over at Home Depot has been feeding me for weeks is true.*

Just as the blue beam found Uncle Silas and bathed him in pure light, he let out one nervous blast of flatulence. The children would have cheered if they were outside, but they weren't.

A half an hour later, Jesse looked outside and saw only the fire dwindling in the night. They figured Uncle Silas had gotten bored and gone home. Karl used the opportunity to teach all of the children the vital importance of fire safety.

Not until the next morning did Chandler, over cereal and toaster pastries, point out the fact that Uncle Silas's truck remained parked in the driveway.

"Yeah, box store jobs. They don't appreciate my creative flair, man! And what business is it of Karl's? It's not like I don't have my own place. Look, I brought the s'mores makings and extra firewood, and I'm just saying we should have a fire, like old times."

"Well, I'm just saying we have all had a long day at the beach, end of story." *Now you sound like Mom*, Uncle Silas noted, *always ending the stories.*

"Well, I'm having a fire!"

"Go ahead," she said, leaving the room, "have your fire."

"I will, you go ahead and watch me!"


Uncle Silas sat beside his fire and looked up. His sister was watching from her bedroom window.

"Well, you're an obedient one, I'll give you that," he muttered. *Karl's masterwork*. Just to spite her, he pulled out an American Spirit and lit it with flair. Her face wrinkled with disgust and disapproval.

He flipped her the bird.

He scanned the other windows. None of them held little faces mournfully watching the flames holding back the shadows for their old Uncle Silas. Who was he kidding? Blue light flashed from every windowpane. Every child plugged into the collective. He could hear the damned beeping and pseudo motocross engine sounds.

*I can't compete with that*, he thought sadly. He looked across the back field and to the New Hampshire woods beyond.

That's when the sky lit up like the Fourth of July on crack. Uncle Silas's mouth fell open, dropping the lit cigarette in his lap.

"Jesus!" he screamed, and then yelped and cuffed

*Adjustments! They talked about their kids as if they were seamstresses on commission, for chrissakes!*

"Kids are kids. Kids make adjustments. That's what they're good for," Uncle Silas explained. "What do you think we did being raised by Mom and Dad? We adjusted."

"Is that what your sister is doing?" Karl muttered, just passing through the kitchen for another glass of purified water. Uncle Silas had never seen someone drink so much damned water.

"Touché, Karl," Uncle Silas muttered back. Jesse flashed her husband an irritated look behind his back. *Oh, yeah, he is irritating a bit, isn't he, sis?*

"Si, your stories are just a little adult, we think."

"Adult? Adult? I mean, sis, I'm not giving them blow by blow descriptions of *Debbie Does Dallas*!"

"They are a bit gruesome. Chandler got in trouble repeating some of your stories at school." Uncle Silas suppressed a smile. *A good kid, that boy, but what a god damned name, poor little bastard.* "And the girls have nightmares. They're in bed with us for weeks after one of your stories."

"Hey, what doesn't kill us makes us stronger." Uncle Silas pontificated.

"Ugh, you sound like Dad," Jesse said.

"Take that back!" Uncle Silas demanded.

"Besides, maybe someone has more productive ways of spending his time besides sitting around campfires…" Karl said over his shoulder while leaving the room, like a ninny coward.

"What was that supposed to mean?" Uncle Silas asked, knowing damned well what that was supposed to mean.

"You've lost three jobs in six months," Jesse said, looking for escape routes out of the corners of her eyes.

# UNCLE SILAS SAT AROUND THE CAMPFIRE
*T.L. Barrett*

Uncle Silas did not sit around the campfire. You needed others to sit around the damned campfire, but oh no, his little sis, Jesse, and her uptight dork for a husband, Karl, had seen to that.

"What, are the kids too big for campfires, now?" Uncle Silas had asked of his nephew and nieces. Uncle Silas's and Jesse's sister, Stephanie, had gone on another bender, so Jesse and Karl had the twins for the summer as well as their own kids. This meant that Uncle Silas was looking golden, for once, but he didn't care. This was too much!

"We just think the twins have been through enough. Even our kids have had to make adjustments…" Jesse said, although Uncle Silas wondered if it wasn't really Karl talking through his dear old meat-puppet of a wife. He kept forgetting to check for the ventriloquist hole in his sister's back, or maybe Karl did it by remote.

killed Helen. Helen was his wife, my mother-in-law, who'd died six years before, after her third stroke.

I didn't argue with him but held the bottom of the container, making sure he didn't spill it on the floor. He grunted, as if to say he'd won this one. I let him. It was the least I could do.

When everyone else is in bed, I serve him whiskey, tell him things I'm sure he'll forget. I tell him I have a seventeen-year-old daughter whom I visit on the last Friday of each month at the Hardee's in Winston-Salem where she works.

Of course, she doesn't know I'm her father, probably only thinks of me as another fat, unhealthy customer who buys too many hamburgers and fries. Sometimes I hold my money a little too long or reach for my change too quickly, just for the chance to touch one of her hands for a second.

And then I sit in the dining room and eat, watching her the whole time, imagining what her life is like—boyfriends and homework and music I'm sure I would hate. I wonder if her mother ever married or told her who her father was. Maybe not me exactly, but that he was her mother's boss at that construction company.

I have no right to know any of these things but that doesn't stop me from wanting to. And it doesn't stop me from wanting to walk up to that counter and tell her who I really am. But, of course, I won't do this. It would help no one.

Instead, I help my half-gone father-in-law pour bleach down the sink and when my wife talks about sending him to a nursing home I say no, we can't do that. It would feel too much like abandonment, something she can't begin to understand but which her father and I have already mastered.

# AN UNDERSTANDING
## *Steve Cushman*

My father-in-law and I never had much use for each other until he came to live with us. He took over our teenage son's bedroom, banished him to the basement. He commanded the remote control; no more college football for me. And he ate all of our food; he seemed to really like my pepperoni Hot Pockets.

But it was the bleach and his dementia that connected us. I found white spots on the carpet in Tyler's bedroom and the hall leading to the bathroom. After a quick search, I located the bottle in the bedroom closet. When I confronted the old man, he denied it, said I was crazy, a bastard that was never good enough for his daughter.

Two hours later, I walked by the bathroom and saw him pouring bleach down the sink.

He turned to me, frightened, like a teenager caught with his hand in his mother's purse.

When I asked why, he said because germs are what

shouts from the shore arose in spurts of laughter and frustration. I couldn't move, and everything I considered vocalizing disappeared inside me, muddled by my gulping heartbeat. Another minute and Tristan remained stock-still. The world slanted around me, pressurizing tightly. None of us spoke, and when I glanced at my hands they were clenched like rocks. And instead of time slowing, it now rushed as Tristan suddenly jumped back over the railing and sat, face in his dry hands. I watched him in his moment of defeat until a dull smack swung me to Ben, who punched at the unforgiving wall of the tower, over and over again.

In the row boat to shore no one spoke. Tristan didn't ask for his shirt back. I held it against my bare stomach. Although I didn't yet know Ben that well I could tell something irretrievable had been lost between the brothers. Already it felt permanent: Ben rowing strong-willed with a swelling right hand, and Tristan hugging himself as if to make sure he was still there. We neared the deserted rocky shore, and all I wanted was for Tristan to lean back and notice me, so I reached up to stroke his windblown hair, which under the sporadic cloud shadow had regained its darker tones.

and a mixture of pine and fish-scent wafted around us. I'd just turned seventeen, straightened my hair and lost some of my early teenage awkwardness. I'd dated before Tristan, but he was the first one that made me proud, and that day I wanted him to turn to me, to touch me, before he jumped. The action would imbue my presence with the event, making it *ours*. But he stepped to his brother instead, who, without a word, slapped him, and with an intensity that overshadowed his youth, said, "Out, not down. Out, T, out." Then, they took each other's faces in their hands and whispered. Nose to nose they stared, mouths moving in turn. I didn't dare move closer. Their faces were serious and focused, and as they pulled away Ben wiped at his eyes. "Fuck him," he said.

More people gathered on the shore, some skipping rocks, some shouting. Tristan's hands fidgeted and he smacked them on his legs. He stepped over the railing and sat on the top bar showing his face to the sun with his eyes closed. In that moment he appeared as a child, the sun instantly bleaching his dirty hair blonde, his relaxed face lost in possibility. A slight breeze rustled my bangs as I peered at the slim waves tapping far below us against the gray tower. Somewhere down below the surface, massive gears churned and spun the invisible menace.

Tristan stood up and the shore went quiet. I held my breath high in the summer air. He remained motionless, perfectly balanced on the middle bar of the railing. He breathed deeply and exhaled. Then: only the breeze and the stasis of pre and post jump, of intention and story. After half a minute I glanced at Ben who stood, mouth open, as if to speak, while staring at Tristan's unmoving feet. Mangled

# TOUCH ME BEFORE YOU JUMP
*Jesse Goolsby*

The rumor was you'd get sucked into the big turbines at the bottom, but we still rowed out to the tall concrete tower near the dam in the lake, climbed the sturdy ladder, and stood leaning over the railing eyeing the sixty-foot drop.

Others had heard of our plan and scattered along the rocky shore some distance away. There were three of us on the tower and I had no intention of jumping, but Tristan, who I'd just started dating after months of hope, had let it be known that he would. I'll never forget the way his tan body compressed when he removed his shirt, showcasing his thin set abs and the mysterious scar up his side I had yet to touch. Later, I'd see his father's diamond ring do similar damage to his back.

Tristan's younger brother, Ben, with awe-filled eyes, kept reminding him to jump out, not down. The sunlight crackled on the late afternoon water,

I am unable to move, to remove my eyes from it and I don't know how long I stay there, leaning over the roof, staring at that S, screaming, before unknown hands pull me away.

It takes me a minute to realize he's not referring to himself, but to my mother. He does turn then, and I can see how ridiculous he looks in that Superman getup of his. A flash of anger races through me at how embarrassing this will be for me if he goes through with the jump. But this is quickly replaced by the shame of having such a thought. Mostly, though, my eyes fix on that giant S stretched tight across his chest, the color of fresh blood, and it screams mutely the past, drug-hazed words from my father's hospital bed that he says he never meant and which I mostly believe. "See? See what you've done? If only you had come with us."

"Shit, Dad, it was an accident. Tragic, yes, but we can get past it. Now *please* come down. You've got to stop trying to assign blame."

"Why not? There is always blame, son. Always," my father says. "I was the one driving. I was the one looking down. I was the one who didn't steer away from the truck in time. So I was the one who should've died. We've been through this a million times, Garrett. How many doctors have said, in fact, I shouldn't be alive? That I must be superhuman to have survived?" He swivels to face me, extending his arms so I can see fully his costume. Superman, gray-haired with a beer belly. "Well, here I am. And if I *am* Superman, then I can't get hurt, right?"

He moves so fast I cannot react. In one motion he turns and steps off the roof. I run to the edge and lean over. I catch sight just as he hits the sidewalk. He lands on his back. Our apartment building is ten stories high and he seems so small, yet I can make out the widening halo of blood around his head, which is bent away so that I can't see his face. The only thing I see clearly is that large red S on his chest.

# S

*Ray Morrison*

A sharp, stiff wind cuts across the rooftop, pressing my father's cape flat against his back. He is standing on top of the short, narrow wall that rings our apartment building's roof. I see him teeter in the gust and I take a quick step toward him, but he holds out his hand to stop me. For twenty minutes, I have been trying to get him to climb down from the ledge, to give up his plan. Another blast of wind raises goosebumps on my bare arms.

When my father turns from me to look down, I use the moment to steal another step closer. I have managed to close the gap to no more than fifteen feet. My best hope, I know, is to keep my father engaged in conversation.

"Are there any people down there?" I ask.

My father lifts his head but doesn't turn toward me. He is staring straight ahead at a thick, pear-shaped cloud moving steadily across the sky. "No, thank God," he says. "I wouldn't want to hurt anyone else."

I sit and sip my gin and watch. I watch as a gent in blue draws close and whispers sweet profanities into her ear. Maybe he's telling her that her eyes are like eclipsed moons, her body is built like a thoroughbred horse, her loins could topple nations. Maybe. Motivated by some primal instinct, I reach for my camera, but discover a bottle in its place. Not wanting to miss such an opportunity, I frame my fingers over her face and take the shot. Miss Carolina glances in my direction a second too long and I smile an inch too wide. To the dismay of her would-be suitors, she excuses herself and glides towards me.

"Do I know you from somewhere?" she says.

"Nope," I say.

"Are you sure?"

"I'm sure."

Making herself comfortable, she takes my glass and pours a drink.

"Do you think I'm pretty?" she says.

"Yes."

"Pretty enough to get paid?"

I pause for a second. "Maybe."

She smiles and places her hand on mine. And maybe that's all she wants. Maybe that's all we want. To be told that we're beautiful, that we're handsome, that we're loved.

# MISS CAROLINA
*Duane David*

It is almost dark when Miss Carolina of '78 drifts into Sadie's with the autumn wind behind her. All innocence has been scraped away, leaving something that's dark, fierce, mature. No longer queen of the Old Tar-heel Palmetto State, she has traded her evening gown for something less elegant. Her scuffed stilettos strike the tiled floor, as she heads for the booth only a few feet away.

She slides to the center of the table with a sort of faded grace and places the napkin over her lap and waits. As if on cue, the old cronies at the nearby bar refill their drinks and flock to her the way photographers flock to their prized cover story. I should know. I used to be one of them. I wonder if she remembers that night we shared. That night the press buzzed and hummed around her, flashing our tiny camera bulbs like dancing fireflies. A somebody surrounded by nobodies. I wonder if she remembers me.

truck begins to work its eerie magic. The rear of the Oldsmobile seems suddenly light, levitational, and the whole day is sun. A cab driver who's been stuck in traffic next to us for the last fifteen minutes looks in my direction and shrugs his shoulders, *Whatugonnado*, and I shrug mine as well, and both of us are thinking the same ridiculous thought, *I couldn't have embarked on this journey alone, much less endured it, what a blessing you were with me.*

The tow truck team even gets a small round of applause, or what passes for applause in these situations. The driver sticks out his arm and waves. It is formal, this wave, a salutary acknowledgement, at once humble and lofty. It reminds me of Prince Charles waving to the crowds when he has just cut a ceremonial ribbon or turned the first spade of earth at a groundbreaking, as if he is saying, "It gives me great pleasure to do this today."

Finally the truck leaves with the Oldsmobile in tow and the rest of the traffic creeps forward. Within an instant, it seems, the day is ahead and the ordeal faced by all travelers from time immemorial has been endured and transcended. Traffic is flowing as easily as pedal boats on a pond, and at more or less that same pace, two or three miles per hour, but flowing. That's the important thing to us all, that it's flowing again. Then the woman who has abandoned her car to begin with steps forward from beneath a Bed, Bath & Beyond awning, as if owning up at last, only to toss her head like a colt, discard her empty root beer can into a wire trash basket with a bank shot, and give the rest of us the finger as we pass.

we are sitting on a bomb, a trio of compressed tanks of bottled hydrogen surrounding nitroglycerine, ammonium nitrate dynamite, smokeless powder, but simply because we are stuck in traffic. We are on the west side, stuck in traffic on Seventh Avenue behind an ancient Oldsmobile convertible with New Jersey plates that has been foolishly abandoned. Thankfully a pair of tow truck drivers are working with grim efficiency at getting it off the street. A woman has abandoned it in the worst of possible options, in a lane marked KEEP THIS LANE FREE. Traffic glued solid almost immediately as cars farther back pulled into the KEEP THIS LANE FREE lane thinking they'd avoid the problem. Things compounded after that. The whole thing has taken on an unpleasant tone.

Cab drivers have been blowing their horns and sticking their heads out and cursing the heavens at least as loudly as Ahab cursed his great white whale, and there is that sense of testosterone in the air you feel anywhere in the world when men see a woman doing something unspeakably spoiled or unforgivably stupid. But now that the tow truck team is fastening cables to its rather massive Oldsmobile rear, there is something approaching a renewal of the faith, one of those small fraternal moments in which all men are one.

There has been some drizzle, which has only made the waiting worse. Not to mention the chill. You can feel the chill of a February from the Hudson before you feel it anywhere else in Manhattan, and there have been periods during the delay when Seventh Avenue has seemed to be nothing more than a muddy lowland field deep in winter's grip. That's soon forgotten once the winch on the tow

# RAMZI YOUSEF STUCK IN TRAFFIC
*Jay Boyer*

It's February 26, 1993, and the plan is to park beneath the North Tower of the World Trade Center. We are sitting on enough explosive charge to break through four sublevels of concrete beneath the North Tower's parking garage, enough to break the moorings of the tower itself, then bring down the South Tower as its sister implodes, all of this before the lunch hour so the towers will be full. But none of that matters half so much as the foolishness of women.

My name is Ramzi Yousef and the day began with the yellow Ryder truck I'm in. It was parked on Nicole Pickett Avenue, where I live in Jersey City, New Jersey. My Jordanian brother Eyad Ismoil was behind the wheel and he called me out with a toot of its horn, then three short taps, almost playful, one for each tank of the hydrogen. My brother's still behind the wheel, but looking agitated, not because

# OUTSIDE STURGIS
## *Barbara Henning*

    Women come here often with their tents, the park manager says. In Afghanistan, three decades of war have left one million widows with only the possibility of prostitution, begging or suicide. The sound of crickets and then I fall asleep deeply. Slide    turn    come down    ring me    onward. Sometimes it's too hot or too cold and the world is full of snow or dust storms or the warlords who control the women and ninety-three percent of the world's illicit opium. But we need a place to put our computers. Yeah, it's green now but there's been a drought for ten years. Not a soul on this highway at six-thirty a.m. Then standing in the middle of a herd of cows, I see a man wearing a cowboy hat. With the coming of the ranchers and big herds in Arizona, with the coming of fences and the accumulation of wealth, hunters became raiders. Slide    turn    come down    ring me    onward.

after them. He hoped they wouldn't catch them and he hoped everyone made it safely, but those hopes unnerved him enough to jostle him from sleep.

The light was creeping over the eastern edges of the Earth, casting shadows in the west. It was already getting hot, which didn't help the often suffocating still, dry air. In his dreams, Uncle Napi heard the horses of the trackers whinny, but once awake, he heard them again. Then he heard shouting.

He sprang to his knees, looking in every direction; there was no telling where the hunters were coming from. He woke everyone up and pointed to an outcropping of small caves in a narrow red canyon almost sixty yards away. Everyone packed up what little they had, strapped it to their backs, and sprinted without looking back.

Uncle Napi ran behind everyone, despite being the most physically fit, to ensure no one fell behind. He watched the open desert field over his shoulder, expecting the bounty hunters to come galloping over the hills shooting.

The group reached the entrance to the caves and squeezed inside. The noises grew louder. Someone was approaching. Trying to keep their gasps for air quiet, everyone held their breath as the horses and their bloodthirsty riders slowly trotted by the caves. Uncle Napi watched them pass one by one by one.

He sneezed.

Everyone in the cave glared at him, wide eyed, like lifeless granite statues.

Off in the distance, Uncle Napi thought he heard a coyote howling.

know. Now get some sleep because we have another long day tomorrow. And don't tell me you're not tired, because I had to carry you those last few miles," he said with a grin looking at his nephew. He covered the boy with a small threadbare blanket before going in search of brush and twigs for the fire. Wandering around alone in the desert at night wasn't the wisest thing to do, but the fire needed to be kept alive because it was keeping the group alive.

When he got back his nephew was sound asleep, so he was careful when adding to the crackling flames. He glanced at his sleeping companions and yawned; he hadn't slept in two days. Glancing at the dark horizon, he figured that he could sleep a few hours before the unrelenting sun resumed its journey through the daytime sky.

Before he could settle down, there was a rustle nearby. Rifle in hand, Uncle Napi glanced around and stared into a pair of glowing yellow eyes floating in the darkness a few yards away. The eyes moved together, left and right, up and down, approaching the fire at a slow, cautious pace. When it got close enough, he could see the grey mangy fur and the waging tongue hanging out of the starving, salivating jowls.

"Coyote the Trickster, we mean you no harm. We will be gone soon enough," he said. The creature gulped up some nearby scraps of meat from a carcass in the sand, glanced in the direction of the fire once more, and satisfied there wasn't anything else worth eating, disappeared into the oblivion of the night. Uncle Napi yawned again as he laid down.

He dreamed about Coyote's presence, and what it meant for their journey into the mountains. Uncle Napi dreamed about the bounty hunters chasing

# RUN, NOT HIDE
*Trevor Tomko*

They huddled around the fire close together, hiding behind a large protruding boulder to get away from the evening's blustery winds. The small group of Chiricahua Apache had sweated all day in the hot desert sun, running through the endless, scorching landscape, and now they were resting for the night under the silent sparkling starlight. For once, they weren't running. They were a malnourished bunch, but their hunger for living propelled their every step forward. The children, the elderly, and most of the adults were asleep except for two.

"Uncle Napi, why are those men chasing after us?"

"Don't trouble yourself with them."

"Why?"

"So young and so persistent."

"But why? Is it true they'll take our scalps if they catch us?"

"They are bad men and that's all you need to

Malone Road to the place we agreed to meet.

One night of course, he didn't arrive.

Bundled into the back of an unmarked van, he was taken to a derelict garage on the way to the Ardoyne, hooded, and shot in the leg.

The limp became part of him after a while. But the barked orders never left him. Nor the trembling fear. The pain that still wakens him. The moment he understood what life meant.

For both of us now, all these thudding years later, history lies like a drunk across our stomachs.

For him, history is forever. It will always be what might have been.

And at night, it is as though he is still a runner, taking to those ugly streets under the dirty lights, through which he runs in the joy of his youth, naked, pale, the ghost of himself, pursued by a bullet.

# A CLEAN BREAK
*Michael Spring*

We were young, impetuous, stupid. It was the 1970s. We were in Belfast.

Guns poked around corners. Death was a casual visitor.

Cramming our minds with things we hardly understood, poring over books, searching for dates, for reasons why the times were as they were, we took advantage of youth and ourselves, loved at random, uncritically, too much.

Our bodies were pale, unused to sunlight. We were like puppets, driven by relentless forces erupting within us.

Why Gerry should want to streak through the scarred, uncompromising streets of that city, I still have no idea.

He told me, much later, that he wanted a break from history. But history was much too close to ignore.

I used to hold his clothes. Then I would walk up

# 1976
*Jason Sinclair Long*

Johnny Woods from Philly beat the shit out of me the day he started at our school.

I vowed revenge and got it, but not how you think.

For years I failed to sabotage everything in his life.

Finally, bigger forces took care of it for me.

Word spread fast: Johnny had reached into the washing machine at the wrong time.

Agitator took his arm off at the shoulder.

Wish I could've just kicked his ass or something instead.

David had tried to understand, but the meaning of his mother's words escaped him, until his first mission outside Israel. He had been ordered to assassinate a Palestinian living in Beirut. The man had his son with him all the time. David stalked him as long as he dared, then killed the father in front of the boy. The next day, as he was packing to leave the safe-house, his mother's voice came to him so clearly he thought she was in the room. "Can't you see the dirt?"

Before she died she had given him the cloth and told him to carry it with him as a reminder. "A reminder of what?" he'd asked.

"Nothing must ever be out of order. That's how they get you."

So he had pulled the cloth out of his pocket, the only thing that he hadn't thrown into the fire. "If your house is clean," he'd said aloud as he started wiping down the room in Beirut, "your life is in order."

Now, thirty-five years later, he was still cleaning. *But you forgot something, Eema. You forgot to tell me that if my house is clean and my life in order, I'd feel safe.*

fond of saying, bite him in the ass.

He brought out a cloth, a square bit of black and white striped cotton, so faded the two colors were almost indistinguishable. With the same precision he used to plan an operation, systematically, right to left, he wiped every surface he might have touched.

When he finished bits of debris clung to the fibers. He shook the cloth over a wastebasket, careful that none of the dirt escaped back into the room. "Cleanliness is more important than anything. If your house is clean, your life is in order," his mother said as she held out the same cloth and told him to clean the room where he and Yoni had been playing.

With his eight-year-old eyes, he had scanned the small space and saw only a game board and chess pieces lying on the table. He put them away and then announced he was done.

His mother rubbed the table with the cloth and held it up to his face. Her pupils were dilated, her voice harsh. "Look. Look at that dirt."

He peered at the cloth. "I don't see anything."

She grabbed the back of his head and pushed it down so his nose almost touched the material. "It's there right in front of you. Are you blind?"

He'd taken the cloth and while his mother watched, he wiped down every surface in the room. When his father came in later that evening he told him what his mother had made him do. "She's crazy," David had said.

"Crazy? Of course, she's crazy. That cloth she gave you is cut from the dress she wore in Auschwitz. She saved it! She saved her camp dress! Can you believe that?" Then his father sighed. "But then how could she... me... all who survived not be crazy? We'd have to be crazy not to be crazy."

During one of the many nights he could not sleep, he had decided it was vital to his understanding of the universe to recall the exact number of suitcases he had packed in his thirty-one years as Mossad. He lost count after six-hundred and twenty-two.

He began to gather his things. Two pairs of khaki pants and gray gabardine slacks first. Then the matching gabardine jacket, its sleeves stuffed with paper to prevent creasing. He zipped the suit carrier and turned his attention to a small leather suitcase. Methodically he removed his shirts from hangers and carefully folded them in a neat pile on the bed. He lined the bottom of the case with his underwear and socks, and then laid the shirts on top. His two silk ties were placed on the shirts as if they were part of a display. He left space for a shaving kit that didn't hold the expected toiletries.

Toothpaste, toothbrush, razor blades, deodorant, shampoo or any other hygiene products were purchased in a pharmacy and then thrown away before he checked out. Everything he wore or used had "Made in the USA" stamped on it. If anyone searched his room they would find nothing that marked him as Israeli.

Before fitting the bag in place, he extracted a roll of bills. He divided it in half, placing each pile into a zippered pouch sewn into the lining of his jacket.

Eleven thirty-one. He picked up his 9mm Glock from the nightstand and slipped it into the space between the small of his back and the waistband of his pants. Finally, he pulled on a pair of surgical gloves and began the room check. He knew he hadn't forgotten anything, yet this habit was hard to break. Every drawer and cabinet had to be searched, nothing left behind that could, as Americans were

# DAVID
## *Johanna Gallers*

David Ben Ya'akov opened the drapes of his Beverly Wilshire hotel room and lifted his face to the sunlight. Images of fig trees at Bet Ya'akov, their branches reaching toward the sun, filled his mind.

*Bet Ya'akov.* Why did he think of the place today? He hadn't been there in forty years. Before he left, he burned his parents' papers and photographs, their furniture and clothes. Nothing of them remained. He had rid himself of family memories and emerged from their ashes reborn as David Ben Ya'akov, child of a place, not of people. He would be part of Israel's future. And he was. Now he was about to become part of its past.

He opened his eyes. Instead of fig trees his gaze fixed on the tiny cars fifteen stories below his window. He checked his watch. A sharp pang in his stomach told him to stop thinking and finish packing. He hadn't eaten anything yet and his ulcer was not enjoying the remnants of last night's wine.

in me and the wind whipped my eyes into tears as I thought about returning to the warm apartment and the worried faces of my daughters. I was back at the butcher shop where they had just pulled the shutters closed and for a moment I considered going in and explaining what had happened, but I'd never asked for charity in my life and I wasn't going to start now, so I walked towards home, dawdling, still looking down, hoping against hope that the fish would flicker into my line of vision.

As I saw the lights of my apartment, I guessed that someone else had probably found the fish and was cooking it right now and the words "Oy vey ist mere" ran through my mind, which means 'oh woe is me' in Yiddish, but I did not speak them aloud for I have known woe and this was just a lost fish. So, I squared my shoulders against the last gust of wind as I walked in the front door and headed for my apartment. I knew that in my kitchen I would find something to feed my family.

The kosher butcher was only two blocks away and by walking in a large square I could go to the produce stand for vegetables, the bakery for bread, the grocer for odds and ends and finally the butcher, to find something we could all eat for dinner with whatever money I had left. The requirement for meat in those days was that it had to be good for at least two meals: a chicken might do the trick, the stock I could make from it would be good for soup, with matzo balls it might even do for three meals. When I got to the butcher, though, a desire for fish overwhelmed me as I looked into the case and saw a large Lake Superior white fish, my daughters' favorite. This too could be made into stock, which would satisfy the two-meal requirement. I counted the money I had left, just enough for the fish, and when the butcher smiled and asked, "What for you today, Mrs. Kohn?" I pointed to the fish shining in the case and he carefully wrapped it in a newspaper from yesterday and I rearranged my other bundles and headed back into the graying, gusty evening.

When I arrived home and my daughters helped with the unwrapping and putting away of my various packages, I nudged the newspaper to the side, waiting to unwrap it last for them, to see the delight in their faces. Fish was expensive and whitefish was their favorite. As I unraveled the paper I realized that something was wrong. The fish was gone, leaving the newspaper smelling only vaguely of once-fish. I gave a cry of anguish and hurried to check the other parcels and then the foyer and then the hallway of our apartment building, the front door that I had struggled to open with my arms full, until I was back down the street and almost to the corner, my eyes scanning the dirty snow for that flash of silver. Panic welled up

# IT GOT AWAY
*Leah Rogin-Roper*

It was the year Sidney died of meningitis, taking with him all of the golden-curled hopes of prosperity for our family. It was the year the stock market crashed and the year my own husband's hair went grey overnight, and he too was gone within weeks. It was the year we had to cover the piano in mourning, a Jewish custom, until we had to uncover it so my daughters could teach piano lessons, our only source of income.

It was the year I realized how hard life could be and I stopped being afraid. After all that happened that year, how could life still hurt me?

It was one of those particularly windy winter days that earn Chicago its nickname when I collected my daughters' teaching money for the week and headed out to do the shopping. I would have taken one of them with me, but Hilda was studying hard for school and Harriet was teaching a lesson. Besides, when the wind blows that cold, it does no good to share it.

Billy turned to his sister. "Just a bit," she said.

"Once I stood on a rusty nail and had to go to the doctor and get a tentinus needle, didn't I, Debbie?"

"Tetanus," the girl corrected patiently.

Mr. Brown shook his head in disbelief as he held out his hand for the string-bags and started to pack the groceries.

"I don't know who will look after him next year when I go back to school. It's my birthday today and I'm six. I'll be in Grade Two after the holidays. Mum's going to make my favourite for tea—stewed apricots and custard."

Mr. Brown looked at the three items he had pushed to the side and packed them in the bags with the other goods.

"Well, Happy Birthday," he said, as he came round the counter to help settle the bags on the small bony shoulders. "Wait a minute." He took two red-and-white bulls-eyes from the jar and presented one to each of the children.

"Thank you," they said in unison and turned to go. The little girl put hers in her mouth and her cheek bulged around the lolly. Billy carefully licked his as his sister reached back and took his free hand.

"You forgot to tell him about the time I nearly stood on the snake," he said.

Debbie nodded. "You'd better put that in your mouth or you'll be getting all sticky," she said.

Mr. Brown put the account book back on the shelf and sighed. So many families in the district were finding it hard since the closure of the mill. Next time the kids came in he must remember to bring the conversation round to snakes.

Mr. Brown smoothed out the paper on the corner of the bench and noted the items written there. He weighed the potatoes, sugar, flour and other necessities and gathered them on the counter. The children watched his every move, wide-eyed and grave.

Then the shopkeeper took down an account book from a shelf and opened it. He frowned briefly at the tally already recorded there, pushed to one side some of the goods assembled before him—half a pound of dried apricots, custard powder, one pound of broken biscuits—and began to write with a stubby pencil.

He looked up at the children. "What have you been doing to yourself, champ?" he asked the little boy, indicating where a large piece of plaster was partly concealed by an uneven fringe of hair. The boy instinctively put his hand to his forehead and touched the plaster, which was slightly lifted on one corner.

The girl immediately brushed his hand down. "Billy, Mum said to keep it covered. You don't want to get germs in it." She turned to Mr. Brown. "Fell out of the mango tree," she said in a conspiratorial whisper.

Mr. Brown winced and gave a low whistle. "Must have hurt?"

Billy nodded and then pulled up the sleeve of his shirt and turned his shoulder to the man. Mr. Brown leaned over the counter to examine the red scar on the soft white skin.

"That's where he fell down the back steps and landed on the corner of the cement," the little girl confided. "He's rather accident prone I'm afraid."

Mr. Brown nodded. "I can see that. Did you cry?"

# **ACCIDENT PRONE**
## *Margaret Dakin*

The grocer was serving Mrs. Gardiner, one of his best customers, when the two children came into his shop. They stood right up near the glass-fronted counter, quietly waiting 'til he was free to attend to them. The little boy, the top of whose tousled head could just be seen over the counter, had his eyes fixed on the lolly jars. The girl, perhaps two years older than her brother, kept her eyes on the shopkeeper as he moved quickly around gathering items from a list in his hand. Her brown pigtails had been plaited painfully tight, and looked somehow in keeping with the faded dress she wore, which would soon be too small for her. A couple of string-bags were slung on her shoulder.

Finally Mr. Brown was able to turn his attention to the children. "And what can I do for you today, Sir and Madam?" he asked with a small bow. The little girl solemnly handed him the note she was clutching in her hand.

anyway."

"Little too late for that."

"Please don't do this to me. I'll give you anything you want."

"Anything?"

"Yes. Please let me go."

"Go stand against the bin."

Robyn obeyed him. Her bag of groceries lay on the ground a few feet away.

"Drop your pants."

"No."

"Fine." The security guard took a cell phone from his hip pocket, held it facing her, and snapped.

"Nice shot for the police. Caught in action."

"Oh. Please." Robyn undid the snap on her jeans, let them fall, and stood shivering in the dark. She clenched her fists. Dear God, let it be over quick.

The security guard laughed.

Robyn tried to stuff down her feelings of humiliation.

"Forget the police. This one's for me." The security guard held up his cell phone and snapped a shot of Robyn in her underwear, her pants in a heap at the bottom of her legs.

He placed his cell phone back in his hip pocket and paused.

"Pull your pants back up. I don't want you."

"You don't?" Relief flooded her voice.

"Nope. I just wanted to see if I could get you out of those pants."

"You mean I can go now?"

"Yep. Don't forget your groceries."

Robyn sealed her bag and climbed out of the bin, her belly sliding down the front edge of it.

Strong arms caught her as she landed.

"Thanks Dana," she said.

"Not at all," the man said. Robyn turned and found herself looking into the eyes of a security guard. He stood only inches away from her.

"Please let me go." She stared at the red insignia on his navy blue jacket.

She tried to move forward.

The security guard blocked her way. He was broader and several inches taller than she.

"You're on private property removing items which don't belong to you."

"It is just food the store threw away." Where was Dana? She tried to look around him.

"You're trespassing."

"Please, let me go. I'll make it worthwhile for you."

"In what way?"

"I have forty dollars in my purse in the car. I can go and get it for you."

"I am not interested in forty dollars."

"That is all the money I have on me."

"Then, you wouldn't make bail, would you?"

"Please, I have a son."

"What does he say about his mother stealing food in the dark?"

"I am honest. I never stole before. This was in the garbage bin."

"Ever been booked before?"

"No. No. I have never been in any trouble. Please let me go."

"I bet you would make a nice mug shot."

"I will put this all back. I don't really need it

Trader Joe's. It sat in the shadows, barely visible to sight. Dana turned off the car and looked around. "Watch the area around the back." She gestured in that direction.

No one was apparent in the feeble light. Dana took a couple of large black trash bags from the back seat of her car. "Here, you are going to need these. Fill them up fast so we can get out of here."

"Don't you think they have video cameras?"

"At the back of a food store? No."

They got out of the Ford and quickly sprinted across the parking lot and to the back of the store. A large garbage bin came into sight. Dana unraveled her bag. "Help me over the edge." Dana was struggling to get into the giant bin. Robyn placed her hands under her friend's buttocks and pushed her over and into the bin.

"This is great! Pancake mix!" Dana was busy placing items in her bag. "Tuna fish, a can of crushed tomatoes, and chicken broth. What is taking you so long? You should be able to get in. You are taller than me."

Robyn hoisted herself over the edge of bin. She peered at the contents. It was the most sanitary garbage dump she could conceive of. There were mostly canned goods but she did spot a bag of apples and a wrapped head of lettuce. She opened her bag and began to place items in it: vegetable shortening, a can of pumpkin, black beans, Jiffy corn bread mix, and oatmeal.

Dana's bag was full. "I'm going back to the car. It is important to be quick."

"Shh. I heard something."

"There is nothing. Finish up and come on." Dana disappeared into the dark.

# RECYCLED
*Nomi Liron*

"No, Dana. I changed my mind. I don't want to do this."

"It will be alright. No one will know." Dana drove without looking at her.

"I always have rotten luck. I just know I'll get caught."

"You said yourself you need the food."

Robyn was silent. Her unemployment checks were running out and money was tight.

Dana stopped at a red light. "At different times there I have gotten tomato sauce, noodles, pickles… all unopened. Free for the taking. And there is no smell attached to the cartons or cans."

Robyn shivered. It was early in the morning just before dawn. She shuddered at the cold. "Can't we come back some other time? I don't feel right about this."

"No. We're almost there now." Dana's blue Ford Focus pulled into the far right corner of the lot at

"Are you writing about me and chemistry? They're going to think your wife's a freak."

That's not what I'm thinking, I'm thinking they too are turning numbers into reality and finding things don't look so good. But then, what do I know; I work in words, not numbers.

in centimeters. I see the mismatched furniture angled into tight positions. We bought none of this furniture, every piece just a donation from friends moving or leaving. In April we will have to move, but there is nowhere for a family of two and a dog to go. We don't make enough money to rent a house or anything bigger than this and dogs aren't welcomed in the places we can afford. For those places we can afford, I wouldn't occupy without a dog's protection anyway.

In our lives healthcare is a philosophy. We could sell dope to make ends meet, but that is my only hope if things go sour. These are our realities. Only one of us can afford school, she is the lucky one.

"This chemistry class is going to kill me. All I hope to get out of it is that we blow something up."

I laugh. Outside our window the geese and ducks are lying on the ice that covers the phony lake this complex dug with our money. The ducks have their heads buried too, but under feathers. The sky is crimson; the clouds are like sheets of cold steel. The Rocky Mountain air is dry and cold, very cold. I try to put numbers to how cold it might be, but fail. I can put numbers on the envelopes that come through the mail: telephone, fifty-five dollars; electricity, thirty-five dollars; rent... well, we've already gone over that. I can't put numbers on the quality of love. I can't put numbers on the hope we share that things will, nay, must get better.

Thousands of miles away my parents are struggling in Italy; they too must move. It's not looking good for them either, but then, Italy just doesn't have anything available. There are six billion people in the world, many don't have homes, but it seems to me the rest of us are just on the verge of joining them.

# A NUMBER ON REALITY
*Bryan Jansing*

My wife is behind me with her chemistry book open, her head buried in another world. Every once in a while she breaks the silence.

"Light travels three million meters per second."

I stand up and stride across the room in three-foot paces that I count out loud in one-second intervals.

"Now if I could do that three million times faster, I could go the speed of light too."

We refill our coffee mugs, share a smile or two and return to our work.

Our apartment is a tiny, 488-square-foot box; nothing fits and everything is crammed into a spot, including our Labrador. We pay almost two dollars a square foot and the rent will go up if we stay. We hate this apartment.

"One inch is 2.54 centimeters," she says.

I look around the apartment and visually pick out inches from the white walls that smother us and turn them into centimeters; the walls are no larger boredom into the coffees I sold. Locals blew inside, spurred towards iced Americanos by the howl of the hot winds outside. They said fire was haloing the valley, skipping freely across canyons as it roared its way to town. As I watched fire trucks screech red and yellow streaks down Woodin Avenue, I crossed my fingers under the counter, rooting for the fire.

my first fiery sip of tequila. I needed my own story. I needed to fall.

When I landed, my feet hit the ground, and I collapsed over the rest of myself like an accordion out of music. My knees smashed knobbed points into my forehead and struck sparks like flint meeting steel. Dazed, I flopped back into the night ivy.

But I'd succeeded. "I'd steal a car for you," he promised, and I swooned for this declaration of love. My hot wet heart plopped eagerly into his hands. And then he went away.

Always another state, another time, another town outside this one. All those tourists must go back to somewhere. In summer I painted nudity into the lake, splashed drunken stars into the sky. Winters, I huddled over maps, warmed my hands on college brochures that promised me a *future*. The winter of my junior year dumped four feet of snow onto already sagging roofs. I filled out applications with the desperation of an avalanche victim. My words could be a small atom of beginning, a flashlight beamed down a dark and twisted road.

In poems, I suicided the boy. I murdered all the stupid, simple boys who dared to carve their initials on my fault lines. I made them jump off cliffs, rob banks and die in raging storms of gunfire. In my stories, they starred as cowards, liars, madmen and anti-heroes. Best of all, I made them ordinary. After a while, they became less real, though they still roamed the streets.

In July new wildfire ate the hills. Ash rained from a black sky. Every morning I drove blearily to work and all morning poured shots of desperate

# SPARKS
## *Amber Ridenour*

I didn't really think that small-town cops would care about a few firecrackers. I guess that wiring children develop in their brains, that light-up switchboard that connects possible action to imminent consequence, had blown fuses in my case. Some important transmission had been lost.

When the air behind Saint Andrew's Church exploded, we were already pounding down the alley, tripping over shoelaces that had stealthily escaped their knots, stumbling on the sharp and evil glitter of bits of broken bottles. Delight and fear tasted like electric pennies, impossible to swallow.

I ran from God, toward Riverwalk Park.

Later, when I flung myself off the roof of the same church, I called it my "fall from grace." I had been panting to impress this beautiful and dirty boy who stole transmissions from parked Suburbans to get money for crack. He was my Hunter S. Thompson, help but feel sorry for the haphazard neglect heaped upon them. They cower there in back, knowing they will not be taken out again until a bag is filled for Goodwill, or, God forbid, for the trash. They've heard horror stories from the serviceable sandals about piles upon piles of shoes tossed willy-nilly into the dumpster, and with no one to wear them, it seems likely to be their fate.

They are bored, all of them, with each other and with themselves and their abandoned lives. No newcomers have been added to their flock for years now, it seems. Their seductiveness, their flashiness, their very value is diminished by familiarity and by disuse. Beside each other's faded beauty they appear even more faded.

Ever hopeful, the jaunty flats with silk flowers at the toes fluff their finery when footsteps approach. Others push forward or cringe back into the depths, as their nature require. Shy gray loafers, worn down at the heel, move into shadow, too tired to want an outing. Gold sandals try desperately to work up a bit of shine, a remembrance of glamour. Flip flops bounce up and down and smile, as is their nature, though they were added on a whim, and have only been taken out once or twice since. Naturalizers straighten themselves, practical as always, preparing themselves for work.

The closet door opens, a bathrobe is pulled down from the rod, and the door closes again on their hopes. The ratty pink slippers remain out, and suddenly all are aware of jealousy, perhaps, but also relief. They are rarely worn, and may at times be bored, but the pink slippers must endure the sadness beyond the closet doors, day after day, with hardly a break.

# SHOES
*Christy Strick*

The shoes stand in formation in her closet, some side by side, others heel to toe. "Pick me," tap the dancing shoes. "It's been too long." The strappy red sandals standing tall in back, once so confident, have given up hope, and no longer try to seduce their way out. Runners and walkers and tennis shoes fidget nervously—they've seen the golf shoes thrown into a bin with others for a yard sale, and know it's only a matter of time. Gone too are the handsome hiking boots, and the flashy suede knee boots, and so many others. "I feel so useless," a pair of platform sandals moans. The black sturdy pumps only nod, sad for the others but glad to still be occasionally in demand. The ratty pink slippers are the only ones to leave regularly, sometimes not coming back into the closet for days at a time.

Pushed into the far back corner, segregated from the others, are discarded wing tips and loafers, larger, less dainty and congenial than hers. These are not neatly lined up, but piled, and a shoe can't outside, get the cake, its frosting melted, exposing the chocolate underneath, and throw it away without taking a bite. As if this gesture could make it so the day's events hadn't happened. When you return to Stan's bedroom and climb in next to his snoring body you are still restless despite your aching limbs. Something is still wrong. And as you play back the last couple hours in your mind it hits you: you should've buried the cake, too.

outdated shag carpet. You understand that its belly will not feel warm to the touch but you still expect it to surprise you and open its eyes and commence licking your face. You wonder if dogs have last thoughts like which fire hydrant it had covered with the most piss. You touch a clump of its dirt matted hair and the smudges bring to life the fingerprint patterns on your hand. You brush the dirt off on your jeans not realizing the futility your action has considering what will come next.

In the kitchen you spot the open bottle of whisky and look for the top but you can't account for its whereabouts. A couple of inches of amber liquid rest inside the glass and you dispose of them down the sink, but not before helping yourself to one swallow. As you walk out the back door you try to remember whether Stan keeps the shovel in the shed or the garage. In the shed you locate the shovel and a pair of gloves, although the gloves are much too large and would only slow you down. You scan the backyard for a suitable place and your eyes rest upon one hole that is slightly larger than the others Rufus has dug and decide to start there. Somehow you can't ignore the irony of how the dog began digging what would later become its grave.

You have never realized how long it takes to carve out a space large enough for burial. In the hours to come your hands will blister as you push the shovel into the earth and use its blade to break apart so many tree roots. You pause in your mission only to check on Stan, pull back his hair while he vomits three times, and send him to bed after giving him ginger ale to remove the awful taste he has in his mouth.

Later, once you are sure he is asleep, you will go

# BURIAL
## *John Abbot*

You pull up to the house and know immediately that something is wrong. The dog is not outside. It doesn't rush toward you from whatever hole it was digging to jump up and place its front paws on the ivy-covered chain link fence. You see Stan sitting on his steps, his face buried in those huge oil streaked hands. Hands that you insist he wash clean before he touches you down there. You hear his sobs as you approach. You know he hears you but refuses to look up and let you see his tear stained face.

On the seat next to you is a cake you made for Stan. It is a very simple, one layer, chocolate cake with white frosting. At first you had thought of writing on it. Something like, *Congrats, the first year is the hardest.* Instead, you kept it clean to represent his sobriety. It is hot out and the cake will surely melt if you leave it in the car, but it seems wrong to bring it to him now.

Once inside you stare at the dog lying on the

caring how harshly they clashed (strongly considered because I was thinking that eternity is too long a time not to be comfortable); but in the end settling on the pale blue summer dress she wore on our first date, a picnic on a hilltop a short drive from school, selected when I remembered how I remarked that the color matched the sky that day—and not surprisingly *this* day—because by choosing that dress, I told myself out loud, that since that was the first day my life truly began, it fit some cosmic sense of symmetry that nothing else would be appropriate, and so listening to the soft whir of the motor that drives the lowering device it is like I can see right through the polished mahogany to see her lying in that dress, made young again by some secret magic the cotton holds, and the memory evokes the taste of the potato salad she'd been so proud that she made herself for the first time and had fed to me with a plastic spoon, laughing when I teased her that it had way too much mayonnaise, but not laughing well enough to hide in those exquisite green eyes the hurt my careless joke had caused, a hurt that caused a pinch in my heart I'd always remember; the same pinch, in fact, I feel now when I hear the whirring stop with a thump so hard it causes me to gasp, not because it startles me, but because for a moment I fear she has been hurt by it, only to be so caught by the absurdity of that notion it triggers giggling, then laughing, and for how long I cannot say, but it is, I hope, only seconds, but turns out—I'm told later—for much, much longer.

# **LOWERING**
## *Ray Morrison*

In one agonizingly long span of seconds—minutes I'm told later—I stand in mocking sunshine, distracted by an awareness of a disparity beneath my shoes—solid ground under the heels; soft, yielding upturned soil below my toes—watching her descent, an unaccustomed tie pinching my sweating neck, the very tie I selected in haste hours before when I dressed in complete, comforting darkness, contrasting the importance applied to picking out what she would wear, a process which took more than two days, having to select from so many things she liked and looked so good in, narrowing the options down to the sleeveless black dress she wore on the day I was admitted to the bar, taking my oath but unable to keep my eyes off her, realizing at that moment I was going to ask her to marry me that very night; or her favorite lounging clothes, hot pink sweatpants with the hole in the left knee that she always coupled with her orange Virginia Tech sweatshirt without

Aunt Ellie was. This man might have been one of her husbands. She had a lot of husbands, I think. Not like us. But I don't know.

Did I never tell you that? You could do something like that at my funeral. If I die first. You could.

## **YOU COULD**
*Lee Griffith*

Did I ever tell you about my great aunt Ellie's funeral? I was just a little girl. I peeked behind a curtain at the funeral home and saw a man reach into the casket and clasp Aunt Ellie's chest with both hands. I walked up behind him and saw how he had slipped underneath her bodice and held each breast. I must have stood on my tiptoes, or maybe I jumped. I don't know. His shoulders shook, but he wasn't making any noise. He bent down and put his cheek against hers. When he stood up, he left his hands in place, right there on her chest—inside her dress! He didn't move them for a while until, finally, he did. He slid them out, straightened her dress and smoothed the fabric. Then he turned and put his hand on my shoulder like he had known I was there the whole time. He led me back into the room where everybody was talking, not in hushed tones like you might think, but smiling and laughing. No one noticed us coming in from the other room where

**EVERYONE ENJOYED THE BUFFET AT THE CHEF'S WIFE'S WAKE UNTIL THAT AWKWARD MOMENT WHEN THE NEIGHBOR'S DOG DISTURBED THE CASKET, SPILLING LITTLE YELLOW IOUs ALL OVER THE BORROWED CARPET**

*Travis Macdonald*

Still, you have to admit it was a beautiful eulogy.

# SIDE B
## GROWLING COWBOYS CAN'T STEAL MEMORIES

| Title | Author | Page |
|---|---|---|
| AN UNDERSTANDING | *Steve Cushman* | 49 |
| UNCLE SILAS SAT AROUND THE CAMPFIRE | *T.L. Barrett* | 51 |
| STAGES | *Marvin Shackelford* | 55 |
| THE UNDERSTUDY | *Katharyn Grant* | 58 |
| THE FAILURE | *Marvin Shackelford* | 60 |
| REVERSE TRIGGERS | *Matt Siegel* | 63 |
| LESSONS | *Jackie Davis-Martin* | 66 |
| ROAD RAGE | *Corey Lee Lewis* | 70 |
| WAKE UP WITH ME IN THE RADISSON | *Dawn Sueoka* | 72 |
| RICHARD GERE EFFIGY | *Rob Geisen* | 74 |
| DRAWN FROM LIFE | *Lee Upton* | 79 |
| NEVER INTENDED | *Charles Rutter* | 83 |
| DONNY AND MARIE OSMOND BARBIE | *Nancy Stohlman* | 86 |
| FAIRY TAIL | *Diane Klammer* | 88 |
| A TRAVELER IN WINTER | *Faye Kicknosway* | 92 |
| THIS IS WAR | *Sharon Goldner* | 94 |
| DODO | *Daniel W. Davis* | 98 |
| THE LAST LAUGH | *Janet Yung* | 101 |
| EVIDENCE | *Danielle LaVaque-Manty* | 104 |
| THE LUTHIER | *Terry Sanville* | 106 |
| IRIS | *Iris Brilliant* | 110 |
| I FEEL SAFE HERE | *Barbara Henning* | 112 |
| THE RED ROAD | *Toyin Odewunmi* | 114 |
| VICTORIA THE CANNIBAL FISH | *Ben Cheetham* | 118 |
| THE CHICKEN TREE | *Michael Frissore* | 121 |
| THE APPLE TREE | *James Edwards* | 125 |
| REVENGE OF THE PEARS | *Leah Rogin-Roper* | 128 |
| THESE PLANTS | *Nick Oakden* | 130 |
| EPISODES IN THE LIFE OF A BEARDED WOMAN | *Teresa Milbrodt* | 131 |
| MUSH | *Jon Olsen* | 135 |
| GOING BACK | *Kona Morris* | 137 |
| WHITS | *Linh Dinh* | 138 |
| THE BUS RIDER'S TALE | *Patricia Eakins* | 139 |
| THE VIDEOTAPE | *Thomas Clayton* | 141 |
| JESUS AT THE DINER | *JP Vallieres* | 143 |

# CONTENTS

## SIDE B:
## GROWLING COWBOYS CAN'T STEAL MEMORIES

| | |
|---|---:|
| EVERYONE ENJOYED THE BUFFET... >> *Travis Macdonald* | 1 |
| YOU COULD >> *Lee Griffith* | 2 |
| LOWERING >> *Ray Morrison* | 4 |
| BURIAL >> *John Abbot* | 6 |
| SHOES >> *Christy Strick* | 9 |
| SPARKS >> *Amber Ridenour* | 11 |
| A NUMBER ON REALITY >> *Bryan Jansing* | 14 |
| RECYCLED >> *Nomi Liron* | 17 |
| ACCIDENT PRONE >> *Margaret Dakin* | 21 |
| IT GOT AWAY >> *Leah Rogin-Roper* | 24 |
| DAVID >> *Johanna Gallers* | 27 |
| 1976 >> *Jason Sinclair Long* | 31 |
| A CLEAN BREAK >> *Michael Spring* | 32 |
| RUN, NOT HIDE >> *Trevor Tomko* | 34 |
| OUTSIDE STURGIS >> *Barbara Henning* | 37 |
| RAMZI YOUSEF STUCK IN TRAFFIC >> *Jay Boyer* | 38 |
| MISS CAROLINA >> *Duane David* | 41 |
| S >> *Ray Morrison* | 43 |
| TOUCH ME BEFORE YOU JUMP >> *Jesse Goolsby* | 46 |

# FAST FORWARD
## THE MIX TAPE

a collection of flash fiction
*Volume 3*

**EDITED BY**
K. Scott Forman
Kona Morris
& Nancy Stohlman

FF>> Press 2010